Fighting the 360

BRENT PALMER

AuthorHouse™
1663 Liberty Drive
Bloomington, IN 47403
www.authorhouse.com
Phone: 833-262-8899

Because of the dynamic nature of the Internet, any web addresses or links contained in this book may have changed since publication and may no longer be valid. The views expressed in this work are solely those of the author and do not necessarily reflect the views of the publisher, and the publisher hereby disclaims any responsibility for them.

This book is printed on acid-free paper.

ISBN: 978-1-6655-6989-7 (sc)
ISBN: 978-1-6655-6988-0 (e)

Library of Congress Control Number: 2022916309

Print information available on the last page.

Published by AuthorHouse 08/31/2022

author HOUSE®

CONTENTS

1

RAISED BY A SINGLE MOTHER

Crying Son

-The days you told me you would come
*   and you didn't*
-When I kicked those Jordans off, the tears came
*   pouring down*
-The only thing to dry up those tears was
*   when you picked me up for a movie*
-No matter how much money or how many gifts
*   I received on holidays and birthdays,*
-It didn't substitute for lost time
-How I cried because the man wasn't being developed
-How I cried because you weren't at any
*   graduation*
-No football games to cheer me on
-How I cried because I suffered in a world
*   that has no patience for boys*
*   and their problems*
-I know I don't want to cry forever, but Damn!
-I cried many days because of lost time
*   to manhood*

Sincerely: Brent Palmer

Summer of 2000, I was five years old playing around in my grandmother's house in Compton, California. Yeah, the city where you get a foot in your butt if you don't come correct. My life began with my grandmother, mother, cousin, and me. They were raising two Black boys on their own like the 70 percent of Black kids in the United States. We shared the experience of having single parents while living the nightmare that many of us Black kids go through. It was normal because all the kids on the block were like us.

I would play with the kids and ride bikes until my body was exhausted. Those were the days I enjoyed, because it was like an amusement park in the hood: riding bikes, playing hide and go seek, and having water balloon fights with the neighborhood kids. I remember my mom would call me into the house to eat and I would shower and lie down with satisfaction, knowing I had played my butt off.

My cousin was quiet like me, kind of kept to himself. He never really talked much, only when we watched wrestling. Back then, WWE was Called WWF – World Wrestling Federation. I remember every Monday, those were the nights we both got a lot of cardio in, mimicking moves from the Undertaker and Kane. we would climb on the couch while my grandmother was sleeping and jump up and down on the furniture. By that time, our noise would wake her up and she would come into the living room to calm us down, then we would go to bed. Next morning, we would get ready for school…man, those were the days.

Hurting in our community is the norm. We just grow up and bring all this pain into our adult life. Now I understand why my mom and grandmother tried their best to keep us grounded. My mom never allowed me or my cousin to visit other people's house. She was always protective about that.

My dad would come around every blue moon and maybe have a meal, but at the that time, I never really knew what It meant to actually spend time with a father. I never understood it because I never saw my father and mother come together as a family. One time he picked me and mom up and took us out to eat. We went to Hometown Buffet. That was a great moment for me. It made me feel great about myself. That was a time when I didn't see fighting or arguments. Back home, arguments were huge.

Where I'm from, Compton, arguments were the norm amongst those who claimed they were a couple. There were times I would wake up with excitement because I knew commotion would be there to entertain. I was five years old, so It was like watching WWF's "Attitude Era" – plenty of entertainment. We had neighbors that would have an all-out brawl in the middle of the street with their kids watching. Seeing their parents argue like that, trauma built up and had a huge effect on them. Seeing that, kids don't have positive image to model after. Kids went into their adult life with no proper guidance on how to function properly and maintain a good and healthy relationship with a partner.

My birthday would come around early in the summer and honestly, I couldn't wait to eat cake and receive gifts; but something would happen that day. I probably saw my dad for five minutes and then he was gone; no explanation, just gone. I wondered why he did that, but at the time I was more focused on gifts and cake. I would look at my mom's face and I saw the let-down. I just thought she was tired from setting up for my birthday, but I knew that she was just disappointed that my dad didn't stay to celebrate. My grandmother would always cheer me up and call me by my nickname, "Poopy," and that made me feel like a king.

No amount of money could substitute for having to do everything on your own. Having a man around for your child's birthday plays a significant role in feeling appreciated and loved. My mom never really got to enjoy that. She would get money from my dad and she would be happy for a moment, but that moment was soon gone and it was back to normal. I understand money is essential in terms of survival, but money cannot substitute for time, love, and affection. Those things keep us motivated and grounded. Without love, we tend not to think highly of ourselves. That's why many look elsewhere and for validation from cruel world.

Mid-summer, the good kid that everyone seemed to love started making a detour in life. It was like a cloud came over my head. I started not listening like I should, and my mother would say, "I'ma call your dad," but I knew his ass wasn't gonna come. Hell, I barley ever saw him. I guess it was a fear tactic to try to scare me straight. My mom would ask me to do something and I would talk back at times, or my grandmother would ask me to do something and I had the attitude of not wanting to do it.

I remember one time my mother left the house with my grandmother and she asked me to do something…I remember there were clothes folded up and I threw them everywhere with no fear of consequences. My mom came home and dug up in the ass. That was a whooping I will never forget. The belt worked a 9 to 5 that day, but not having a male presence in the house, I felt like I could run the household

When I would play around with friends, I would try to mimic them – mimic acts like talking back and acting hard. I failed terribly and it always led to a belt to my butt. At that time, Compton was really getting a lot of press due to high crime activity, so everybody that lived in the city took pride in it and wanting a piece of the chaos. Drive by shootings, doing drugs out in the open, fights in the middle of the streets – honestly, I never wanted that life because I knew I was a smooth and laid-back kid.

I remember trying to act tough and my mom whooped my behind. HA! Whooping was the best, because after that was the best sleep you ever got, waking up sore from a good nap. The next day, my mom would buy me snacks and tell me not to do that anymore. Hearing it from a woman, I took her seriously, but it always seemed odd to me, not hearing it from a man.

Why is it so hard for men to express their feelings and show emotion to the world? Is it because society will label you soft? As a kid, I was always quiet. It may not seem like I had a great understanding of life, but I did. I always knew I was special, but I was too afraid to display that. At school, I would dress differently. Why? Because I loved my style and no one could tell me different.

At church, I never conformed to the crap that everybody was preaching. I never opened up to people, because I felt no one would understand me. I kept to myself until I was around my friends at school where I would be myself. Church would have youth nights every month. Sometimes there would be bowling. During Men's Day at the church, we would eat and talk about different topics. Going to those things, I felt invisible as a person. I don't know why God made me this way, but it was like His shield was guarding me, protecting me from trouble.

I always had trust issues when dealing with individuals. My dad not being there gave me that PTSD effect. When he would promise me that he would come and then not come, it hurted my feelings. So I made it hard for people to connect with me, it kept me from being close to people, even my own family.

I had a close friend that I met back in elementary school and when I would go over to his house, there would be both of his parents. I would see the love and I would get jealous, because that's what I wanted – a family. Every time I would go over there to play around and play video games, I would not want to go home because I was at peace at their house. That environment made me feel like somebody. His house was where I actually saw a male and female come together and raise a family.

I saw how his parents would cook dinner and prepare the table and we would pray together. It may not seem like much, but seeing that would override any game system. One night, I spent a night at their house and for the first time, I was checked by a man for bad behavior. It threw me off guard because I had never been in a situation like that before. I was caught cursing, so I had to read the bible and wash my mouth out with soap. HA! It was funny to me, but a lesson that needed to be learned. No kid should have a mouth like that at our age.

They would always invite me over to family events, and they made sure that they treated as if I were their own. I remember my mom would try to pick me up, but I knew once I got back home, I would be back in the reality of single parents, so I would try to soak in as much as possible of life at his house before going home. And when I did go home, I felt a dark cloud come back into my head. There was no one to talk to, and I'd hear my mom on the phone talking all night about problems. Those were the days I wished I could call up my dad and we would play board games. Instead, I turned on movies to try to substitute for the other half that I was crying for – a father.

I had another friend. His family would take me with them on road trips to Arizona, and we would go to restaurants and go sight-seeing. That was my first time ever going somewhere with a family. Even though they weren't my real family, they treated me as if I was their own. They would pay for all my expenses and treat me to a nice dinner. We would go around the 4th of July. Those were memoires that I would forever cherish, because they shared those experiences with a kid who never went anywhere with his own family. I didn't feel different, because their spirit was welcoming and they always made sure I was alright.

I remember my friend and his dad and I went for a bike ride in Arizona. That was a time I will never forget - just a father taking time getting exercise was something special to me. We rode for about a couple of hours and honestly, our backs were soaked from the hot Arizona sun. Afterward, we would shower and hit the road to look at what Arizona had to offer.

Heavy Heart

Heart is heavy. I guess seeing the women
in my family not married in love
frustrated me.
I realize the importance of having a strong
family, because it sets the foundation
for the future.
No child should have to go out and learn from
a world that doesn't care about them.
Why are 70 percent of Black people
fucked up? I'm a part of it.
But for the first time, I take full responsibility
for my actions.
I do not look for a quick one-night stand
to fill my emptiness inside.
I do not need to be flashy to be seen or liked.
I am who I am because of the integrity I have
for my true self.
I love Jamaican food, I love to love others,
and I love giving.
All I ask for is peace and joy.
May God continue to give me understanding
and patience.

Experiencing life through trials and tribulations, never once did I learn what It took to be a man, from having an erection, to liking and treating a woman with respect, to learning how to carry myself as a man. I never learned about being competent, paying the rent, or taking care of an entire family, because I saw my mother taking care everything with along with government assistance. All I saw was fornication and short-term goals that led to nowhere in the family, such as toxic relationships, odd jobs, and not wanting more out of life.

One of my mother's brother was the only one in the family who was married and raising his family under a roof that he helped provided. My other uncles were being kicked out and forced to come back home to my grandmother or friend's house until things boiled down. Honestly, I thought it was the women tripping, but when you're not providing and the woman is doing the financing, then she dictates how things will be run.

I was clueless to the types of duties that a man was suppose to handle – vital understanding that would develop as time came. Becoming a man from seeing life in Compton through my family around me made a "sucka" out of me at one point, but now I'm able to live and tell you how I got the fuck out of that mindset. It was the mindset of a man being raised with woman's tendency, not seeing hard work from a man.

Back in 2005, crime was at an all-time high in Compton. We were the #1 murder capital in the United States. At that time, people were proud of that! It made us feel different from any other city. I mean, being from Compton, you knew you were different when we walked into other cities. Every night there was shooting, someone's family member doing crack cocaine to cover up the hurt that hadn't been solved. You could always see in the face of others of how they were tired of the life they were living. Drugs were an escape for the moment.

My mother had friends that would be around the neighborhood, and I would always see a bottle in their hand. They thought they were living, but I knew the smell of that wasn't good. I just looked at them as my mom spoke and they would continue on their day.

Also, the incarceration rate of Black males in the community was going through the roof. I mean, one day you see someone and the next day he's locked up. This was the norm for me. I didn't see men working and coming home to love on their family. Men showed more love to the streets than their own family. The connection between the two triggered me, as I saw that. In my mind, that wasn't right. I felt in my 10-year-old mind that it wasn't right. But to them, they were living the American dream.

Toward the middle of 2005 one of my uncles was released from jail. That was our first meeting. He went to jail before I born. It felt kind of badass to have an uncle come from jail, because jail was where the hard people were. Wrong! It was where those who weren't close to their father ended up. There is no school that promotes going to jail; only in our Black community do we glorify doing time, and not focusing on family.

I once thought going to jail was cool, I mean you come back with big muscles and a macho attitude, but where does that get you? Nowhere. Jobs are nonexistent because of your record; you have to rely on a small check that only gets you so far. I mean, were is the man in that? Grown men making less than $20,000 a year. I saw my uncle move in with a woman and he had no say-so. What can you say when cant fully not provide from a family? I used to think laying up with a woman was cool, and for a long time I wanted to grow up like that, but God was able to save and protect me from that.

You'll learn about the shy, horny, and quiet boy that everybody thought was an angel. This is my time to tell my truth. My name is Brent Donqiuse Palmer. I was born May 23, 1995, in Inglewood, California, to my mother and father. My mother was a nurse/in-home care provider; she took care of elderly people. My dad was a truck driver.

I was added to the 70% of the young Black males in America. Born into the chaos that continues to rise here, where young black males are innocently born into single parent homes and welcomed into a life of chaos and turbulence.

My mom and I lived with my grandmother for about 12 years, until mom moved us to Los Angeles to live on our own. My grandmother was divorced and lived as a single woman in Compton, California. Living with my grandmother was different.

What is usually thought of as the ideal family tradition is having two parent in the home raising a child together. However, I wasn't born into that. Growing up as a young male, I never told my mom my problems or asked her intimate questions. It didn't seem right to ask a woman about those things.

During my infant and teenage years, I would only see dad maybe five times out of the year, and out of those five; sometimes it would be intentional. I'll explain… Sometimes, I might be in the car with my mom to pick up child support, or maybe my mom and I would be in the street and we would see him.

The times we did spend together, we would see a movie and he would drop me off and come inside my mom's house for bit. Then he would go back home to his family.

Can't lie, the best moments of my life were when my dad would pick me up. it was better than going to Disneyland or having a new pair of Jordan 11 shoes. Those are the moments that I would forever cherish because of the way being with him made me feel. It made me feel wanted and loved. Some of the moments I had with my dad were when we would go to the movies and watch scary movies. I would be beside him and whenever a scary part happened, I would get close to him. That gave me a sense of being protected. After the movies, he would buy me anything I wanted to eat. My favorite meal would be Mexican food: tacos with rice and beans and a large lemonade.

I remembered once we were finished eating and were in the car heading back to my house, I would hope time would move slower so I could have more time. However, as soon as I saw my house, it was back to the reality of being raised at home by my single mom.

I always felt soft when I was at home, because I felt like a baby. I always thought men were supposed to be tough. But there were times my dad promised he would pick me up and never showed up, no call or text. I would just cry and lay down, hoping he'd come before dark. Those were the days I made up my mind I would never let my kids down like that when I start my own family.

I remember one time it was close to my birthday and my dad was supposed to pick me up to get an outfit. I was pumped and excited. It was a Friday morning. I was heading to school and all I think about was getting the day over with so I could prepare to be with my dad. When 2:30 p.m. hit, I would run home. Now, I would usually try to stay with friends, but when I knew my dad was coming Saturday morning to pick me up, I had to go home and pick out an outfit so I could be ready.

I woke up Saturday morning with a big smile knowing I was going to be with my dad. I had my Kellogg's Eggo waffle out of the box and some Tampico juice loaded inside my cup. I would be showered and dressed and waiting at the door. But as time went by and the sun turned against me and the nap that I took turned into me lying in the dark with no phone call, I was left with no answers.

That was the saddest day ever, because I knew I had to go to school being disappointed on Monday. I had my whole week crushed and the motivation to do anything was gone. My mom would say ``your dad 'aint shit," but I heard the hurt from her heart. I knew that he had hurt her as well. At that age, we don't fully know what's really going on, but we can always sense when something is not right.

As an adult, I never questioned my father as to why he wasn't there for me while I was growing up; I could only imagine why. As you look deep into the 70 percent of single mothers, you start to wonder if it was a one night stand or maybe he wasn't ready. Anyways, there's a problem in there somewhere that needs to be addressed, because if not, it will continue to go on even when I start a family.

Another time I had with my dad was during Christmas month, that first week he came by to take me shopping at "Toys R Us." That was great feeling. Money became my comfort making up for the time that wasn't spent with me. I became addicted to his pocket. Not in the way of asking all the time, but I learned love through him spending money on me. Never genuine hanging out and sleeping at his house.

Money could never replace the teaching of love. Love is what we have when all else fails. Love ensures that we continue. That's why when people stop trying in the world, they quit because they don't have love to continue to push them. If money was so important, then why do people quit when things get hard? Because the love was never there, and the motivation for what they wanted was never pure. As a kid, I quit on a lot of things because I felt the love for me at home wasn't there. I quit wanting to do well in school because I felt no one cared at home, so I never really tried.

"Mom"

*I guess the absence of a father not only affected
        me, but you as well
As your health declined and the motivation
        to do more was covered up by eating
Sweets became your comfort for your heart
And arguments with me to settle the score
        with my father
Times you were forced to be by yourself
        made you feel like nothing
I was young, so I couldn't help – I could only see
        and suffer
When will time ever heal the brokenness
Will time make your son a better man
        for a woman
I promise to give my family what matters:
        my time
Money and sex cannot make a family,
        but time can build a dynasty
I promise, my beautiful Black family,
        you will have what your daddy
        didn't have.*

During my early years from age 9 to 10, my mother signed me up to play football for our local youth program. I played for a year, but later had to sit out due to being overweight. The only thing my mother taught me was how to clean and keep myself up. She would take me get haircuts and buy smell-good supplies: soap, deodorant, and lotion. But those were the basic essentials that any human being needed. At the time, my mother was working. I never saw my mom with another guy – at least she never brought a guy around me.

When all else failed, she signed me up to play for the youth football team. We practiced at our local neighborhood park Monday through Thursday. I guess it was mom's way of getting me around a male figure. I could not get in tune with the coaches because I never interacted with a man at home, so taking orders from a man that wasn't my dad was difficult. I remember the coaches would talk to my mom about my behavior, but by the look on my mom's face, she didn't have the answers either.

During one practice while we were conditioning, getting ready for our first game, I remember a coach told me to do something and I must of looked at him with this dumbfounded look. I told him what I wasn't going to do! He turned to me with a serious face, and if you ask me, he wanted to punch the shit out of me, but he couldn't. He then went over to the other coaches and whispered to them, but I knew what he was saying.

I felt it was wrong in my heart for a man that I didn't know to tell me what to do, but my attitude at practice was poor, and I knew the coaches wanted to whoop my behind. I'm sure he saw my mom struggling, so he got why my behavior was like that – just a typical kid with no father, so he has trouble taking authority from a man. All the other kids seemed to have the issue, cussing and no respect for men able to be our father.

We would go play other teams that were predominantly white and the atmosphere was totally different. I saw kids with manners and their two parents coming to the game. It was different from what we had. Seeing that, I saw how Compton was in turmoil and other kids were being raised differently.

At an early age, kids have a good understanding of the basic sense of self, meaning children can cognitively think and are able to look at things in their totality. Indeed, it's true that kids know what is going on in terms of awareness. That is why they create the cognitive dissonance between themselves and other people and beliefs. What's so special about this is that our decision is heavily based on the emotions of how people make us feel. For example, many will fall for gossip or theories people throw at them, and at that moment our emotions are aroused and we make decisions based on that moment, not on how we really feel. I knew my mom was struggling raising me, because she could never sit and talk about life essentials that I needed to know to become a man.

In 2004, my mother and I joined Church under our Pastor. I was 9 years old at time of joining. Months in, I became a part of the choir and usher board. Upon joining, I was forced to sing in the choir by my mother. I didn't like it. For one thing, I couldn't sing; two, I thought it was for woman to do. I guess it was my mom doing what other parents did at church, which was put their kids in the choir. Funny story, at first I enjoyed singing in the choir, not because it was something I wanted to do, but it was new and fun at the time. We had an annual day and I remember shouting and singing the highest. People were laughing because I was this young kid having a ball with no full understanding.

I had a couple of bad experiences at church. People use to tease me because of my weight. I thought you went to church to get healed, and people were teasing me, bringing me down. That's why I shut people from church out my life. I was quiet and kept my distance, because the energy I was receiving was not to my liking. I'm not sure my mother knew, but she was so excited to be a part of church, she was blind to what was going on. Or maybe she thought nothing of it.

While going to church my mother met her friend that she had been friends with since her upbringing in Compton. She was such a nice lady. She would always looked out for us, whether it was food or money to help out for a holiday. I always felt the genuine love she shared with me and mom. I'll never forget one Christmas when mom was kind of short on money, she came through to complete my Christmas. She had a great idea of what we were going through.

She was married with a really good job and a house that she paid for on her own. She had two daughters and took care of them really well. I would look at that and feel inspired because that was what I wanted but couldn't get. Her daughter liked me, but I was too afraid to express my feelings toward her. I became distanced from her so I wouldn't be hurt first.

I remember we would go over their house to hang out and she would be all on me and I didn't know what to do. The only thing that was excited was " big man" down there." She tried to be intimate, but I was too shy and nervous.

I would like to personally thank that lady for helping me and my mother out. She would even take us grocery shopping at store with good quailty foods. That was the first time I had ever been to a store that sold a large quantity of foods. I was used to our local food stores in the hood. TV dinners and processed food were my everyday meals. I thought that was good; at least I had a meal.

During Men's Day at church once a month, I honestly didn't know where I fit in. One day I had a piercing in my right ear and a guy asked, "What you doing?" I looked at him with a confused look and asked what was wrong, and he said the earring supposed to go on the left. He said men wear everything on the left. I was so embarrassed that I excused myself to go use the restroom. I had to empty out the tears. I felt like so much less of a man, not knowing something as simple as that. You see how bad I had it. I know it wasn't a big deal, but going out into the world, they would have definitely roasted me for something like that.

It was difficult for me to do something half-heartedly. Walking into church every sunday with a fake smile to cover up this fake image. Walking in, speaking to elderly people, and hearing them say, "He's a good boy." Every time they would say that, my conscience would bother me, because I knew I was just like any other youth, living and making mistakes. Just my handsome face would win people over, I guess.

Also, while going to church, the males in there were kind of bitches to me in way. In spite of being 9 years old, I had a good sense of when shit wasn't right, and every time I would get around the males in church, I could never connect. Also, in my head I was still this guy with a lot of emptiness inside, with no sense of who I was. Being teased my whole life about my weight had a heavy impact on my life. Not hearing a positive image of yourself, you begin to believe and feel what other people think about you, which eventually made me hate myself.

I had four uncles. One was married with children and a home. The other three were living with girlfriends. We were not close, but I would always hear their stories of how their relationship was going through my mom conversation with them through the phone. As a man that didn't know much, I would always pick my uncle's side, but now that I'm older, I know why some of the problems erupted in their relationships. Titles don't mean anything. To be a husband, you need to be emotionally, spiritually, financially, and mentally ready to lead a family, and that wasn't the case for them.

I had an aunt that had two baby daddies. Her first was before I was born, but it didn't work out and her last boyfriend never married her, so my whole life, I never saw a happy married couple. Now I'm in my mid 20's and I have to begin reprogramming my mind and learn what It takes to be a man. Now I know why I struggle with women; when you meet a woman, it's a huge difference when dealing with a girl you are trying to just have relations with versus wanting to build with someone. No, I have not had a real relationship yet, but from my experience, you know when you have a woman or girl. And God will not allow you to get certain things if you're not ready.

Also, I was a shy guy. Never knew why I was always shy, but I guess that's the mystery that you would soon find out. I remember in preschool, this brown-skinned girl would give me kisses on the cheek every morning. I thought it was just being friends, but at that age you just go with the flow. Even middle school and up until college, girls would always call me cute, but I never paid it no mind because I didn't think that way about myself.

I had really deep insecurity about myself because of my weight, and I just never felt wanted. Confidence starts at home from parents. If you don't have that, you will struggle once you leave home and interact with the world. The foundation that our parents set for us at home will set the tone of how we will feel once we leave home and engage with others.

Positive self-image comes from your parents. Those who don't have that image at home tend to lean toward the world for their image; however, that is not what God made us to do. Because God made everyone for their own purpose in life. I believe many children struggle with their image growing up due to lack of parenting at home. It correlates together.

Some children have better relationships with their friends than their own parents. For example, when I would go to school, I would try to be like others and not myself, mainly because my values at home weren't given to me. Consciously, I knew I was making the wrong decisions, because those acts would always begin to bother my conscience. Eventually, though, this behavior will condition your mind to think this is the proper way of thinking.

2 Pac had a slogan called "T.H.U.G L.I.F.E," which stands for "The hate you give to little infants fucks everybody." What a poweful statement that slogan is. What I got from that is your children will become exactly the way you raise them. It's like seasoning chicken. Growing into an adult and learning manhood, you realize the importance of having a strong relationship with your parents. It's the base that you start with to grow from, into the man or woman that you ultimately become for a future husband or wife.

Unfortunately, with the absence of a father, Black men create this separation that causes Black women to develop anger toward them, which continues to spread through the children. I'll explain: The first time I ever saw my mom and dad together, I was 9 years old. He would come over and go into my mom's room and close the door. Now, at that age I was smart enough to know that they could talk in the living room.

My dad was married and my mother was single struggling to pay bills. My dad and mom would still mess around together from time to time. What that psychologically did was damage my image of how a woman should be treated. I saw that at home, so I thought it was right. We look at our parents as this perfect example of how to live. For example, I would go to school looking to have sex with girls. I was freshly in the sixth grade with a hard hat and no idea how to use it. After my mom and dad would finish, I smell the after math – lol. It reminded me of that part in the movie "Boyz N Tha Hood" when Tre was having sex with his girl and the grandmother walk in with the sex smell "stanking" up the house.

I would like to point out how significantly seeing those actions can damage a young male's life. Seeing that, I thought it was okay to treat women like that, but it wasn't. Black males learn early on about sex and other things that don't make you a man once you're grown. At the age of 11 or 12, my penis got hard and I didn't know why it was getting hard. I just knew it was it was bigger than normal. I was at home and my mom was in the living room and I was in the room watching the sex scene from "Baby Boy." Know what I'm talking about? "You gon' make them tacos right" – that part had me going crazy, HA

Watching my mother, I saw the lack of motivation, her self-worth was low, because of lack of love and caring. My mother was an overweight girl and as I got older, I realized how my dad not being there made her feel unworthy to the point of eating a lot and not taking caring of herself. Every time I would get on my mother's nerves, she would always say "You're just like your dad," but I just knew that he hurt her and she was too afraid to express herself. There would be days where it would be toward midnight and she would eat something sweet. I thought it was normal to eat that late, so I joined her. It felt good eating and lying down, while the calories would go into our stomachs.

Being self-motivated starts with self-care. We cannot control how people treat us, but we can control how we treat ourselves. We can control our physical fitness - how we eat, how we work out – and how we dress. We tend to let ourselves go when life hits and we have no motivation to do more.

I say all this to say that when the father is absent and he does not do what a man should do, he breaks up the family structure and that leads to women fending for themselves and kids learning on there own. Children need to see their father working and taking care of their family; it creates an energy that bonds everyone together with love, respect, integrity, and character – all those traits that make you who you are.

Fast forward to high school: I started at Compton Senior High School, where I joined football and met new friends. There, I was able to be around men – coaches that graduated college; also men that were competent in taking care of a family. I never knew what it was like to be yelled at by a man until I started practice. I thought coaches were being mean, but it was tough love. The transition from not experiencing a man at home to being yelled at outside of home was a huge difference.

My manhood was being feminized by my mother; in order words, I was soft. I didn't have that assertiveness and confidence that others displayed around me. I always knew that, but was to embarrassed to ask anybody about it. In 9th grade, I was so pumped to finally be able to play football again; this was my only shot at getting into shape to learn how to be like everybody else.

My first practice was my first time seeing guys with the physique that I wanted. Hanging out with them and hearing the talks they would have about girls and everything, I became very intrigued. Guys were talking about sex, and I was hoping they wouldn't ask me about that, because I didn't have the experience for that conversation. It just made me get more curious and anxious. I would watch porn and I would analyze everything. When my teammates would talk about sex, I would say "Oh yeah, that shit does feel good." Yes, sir, my hand felt good at night. These are the spectator moments that made me feel a part and seen, but I was just running, lying with a boner from watching Ebony Porn.

Being raised by a mom, you'll never learn how to function properly around other men. There, you see how not having a father could cause trouble with males who interact with other males outside of home.

One thing I would give my mom credit for was she never had a man coming in and out of the house; if she was messing with someone I didn't see it. Much respect to her for not allowing me to see that. I'm forever grateful for that. My mom wasn't perfect, and I understand the frustration that may have come up along the way, but she made it happen the best way she knew how.

Message to the Black male in the U.S.: if you don't want to create a family, then don't make a decision that leaves the mother struggling to take care of a child that you helped create. Men are the leaders, not the women, and we have to take responsibility for our actions. If not, then we continue this paradigm of family structures that continue to separate us. As a parent, you cannot tell your children about righteousness unless you're doing the right thing.

One of the most significant things that happened to me was during my senior year of high school. When I met my offensive line coach, he would be tough on me and he always left with motivation quotes that stuck with me - "fight until death." Until this day, I really treat every situation as if it's "to death" no matter how hard the obstacle may seem. It really helps with perseverance and being able to endure some difficult times. That coach was the first time I experienced discipline from a male. Don't know why, but till this day it was the best experience of my life; it would later help create this self-worth of never giving up, no matter how hard the situation and task was.

It's funny because there has been a lot of research that talks about how children excel when they feel loved and cared for. My high school senior year was the first time I felt like someone really cared about me as a human being. Talking to him always made me feel like I could do anything. The world will always try to tear you down with awful remarks. I learned many don't like themselves and use putting you down as a way to make themselves feel better.

Males being raised by their mothers will often grow up with female tendencies. My situation for example: I wasn't seeing my father taking care of the household or spending time with my mother, so growing into adulthood I never understood the importance of being able to take care of family, go to work and pay the bills.

2

LOOKING TO THE WORLD FOR HELP

My Esteem

Where do I get my confidence from
*   when the world sees me as nothing?*
While others get their support from seeing
*   others on their knees*
Home life sucks, no proper support,
*   so we seek support from strangers*
Never learned what it meant to be
*   confident growing up*
I thought having nice things would hide
*   my insecurities*
Every time I bought something, it gave me
*   a "high" that only lasted for a moment*
I guess I learned it from my mom,
*   when my dad dropped off child support*
I used to think everything was good
*   until the money ran low*
*   and it was back to waiting for the 1ˢᵗ*
Now that I'm older, I understand
*   the best feeling I ever had was*
*   spending time with my dad*
Those were times I felt good about myself
Where do I get that feeling again?
Traveling helped me look at life differently

Where do I get my confidence from when the world sees me as nothing and the support at home is not that great? Support I don't money, but emotional and spiritual support. Do I run to social media, or do I begin to create distance between me and my family to find the truth? When doing the opposite in the household, it creates uncomfortable vibes that will have people thinking that you are trying to make them feel inferior to you.

Whenever you do something that hasn't been done at home, family starts to look at you differently. For instance, once I started college and got a passport and started traveling, I saw different things that made me look at life differently – how people live, how people treat others. Most importantly, I saw different cultures. I saw how everyone is affected by racism and living conditions, such as people of the same race wanting to be first. Here in America, being Black you see how the main focus is people in power wanting to see minorities as inferior to them; however, in other countries you see how it's the same thing.

The ideology that I once adopted became dead to me. I saw how people suffered from racism as well as poverty regardless of race. I was humbled by the poor and inspired by the rich and how well both the rich and poor treated me in spite of having a lump sum of money or very little. These are things that are essential to our character, how we carry ourselves when things are in our possession and how we act when life is not fully in our favor. True character never changes no matter what your situation is.

Enhancing your life comes with a lot of confusion amongst those you see every day. Some will take it as you wanting to move on, some will see it as competition. Not in the sense that you're better than them, but you're doing things to better enhance your life so that you won't end up like common people. Being different creates separations. I say that because as I broke away from my family tradition, I started noticing how family and friends would approach and talk to me. I stopped relating to the foolishness that had me thinking the same as them.

Everything started to feel like a lie, and I was fighting those thoughts by getting knowledge from somewhere else. In our community, we learned about the racism that hinders our success. I used to hear at my granny's kitchen table that the white people aren't going to give you shit. And since grade school, I learned that white people were better. My mom once came to school in the fifth grade and talked to my counselor. She wanted my teacher to be white because they teach better. In other words, they know more than colored people.

For a Black kid who didn't know much, this affected me. I'm a Black male; do I fall short of being great? Here I'am a black man watching someone put a man down who looks just like me, but older. You'll see the psychological warfare that plays in your mind. You know in the back of your head you could never be great being yourself.

Black parents had that bad, always encouraging their kids to be taught by whites. I don't mean it in a bad way, but what message are you sending to your kids? How come they can't say that a young Black brother can be a great teacher? In the fifth grade, I had a white teacher, but they were going to transfer me over to one of the Black teachers we had. My mother caught wind of it and stopped it. At that time, I didn't know. I just thought having a white teacher was better. Well, I had the class with my White teacher and felt no difference.

I must say my education was poor in the hood. Teachers were not engaged or motivated to teach anything. More so, it's the lack of skill to teach kids of color. Compton was half Hispanic and half black and most of our teachers were white. They didn't know anything about us except what they saw or heard on TV or radio. So, they had an idea, but no knowledge of the psychology of why there are certain behaviors in our community. You see how all that plays a part in our community – our parents subconsciously put us down without directly telling us, by putting a man's color over his ability to be competent and successful.

Eventually you step out of the house looking for your identity, whether it's being popular, a player, or the smooth dude. My search started in college. I thought college was about having a lot of sex with different women to brag about to your friends. I went to college for the wrong reason.

My first time getting some sweets blew my mind. It was shortly after high school. I watched a lot of porn, so I was ready to do the "nasty". I remember I didn't know what the fuck to do, I just knew my man down there was ready to clock into work. I remember she grabbed me and started kissing on my neck. Shit, I almost bust then. I was wondering what to do, so I mimicked one of the porn stars that I watched frequently and it worked. I mean the way I was handling business, she thought I might have had sex with a 100 girls before her. Ha! If she only knew.

It was a cool experience for my mature mind. I mean, I had to brag to friends with the sex face. You know, the cool eyebrow raised with the extra confidence on your shoulder – *yeah fellas, you know what*

I'm talking about. Wanting to get in between girl's legs was my number 1 mission. I wanted more and it became my agenda to get more.

My first year of college was like an Easter egg hunt for women, but instead of finding eggs, I was trying to find vaginas. Getting vagina was my main focus. I didn't care if I missed an assignment, I was going to find some girl's skirt. Yeah, but that wasn't a great idea. That mentality started to mess with my grades and I didn't want to drop out my first year, so I put my focus back on school and got on track.

I finished my first semester with a 3.6 GPA. What a great moment that was, because I had never received a GPA that high before in all my years of going to school. The closest I came to that way in tenth grade when I received a 3.0 GPA, so it was like a nostalgic moment. I had two female teachers that both taught English Literature, and I had a Human Development teacher that was awesome.

That was the first year that I felt engaged and welcomed into an environment that wasn't judgmental about your learning ability. The way they engaged with me and my class, we all excelled. I had classes with my fellow Tar baby brother and we had a great time helping each other. He went on to do well for the remainder of his college career.

College was great. I mean, I can't complain. There were moments when I thought about quitting, but I didn't. College was my way of showing my high school teachers that I could become a college graduate, because I was true dumbass before college. I just never tried because I had no motivation; I wasn't doing it for anybody but myself. I can recall times where I did assignments and homework just enough to get by, and I was cool with that. I was scared to reach for my full potential, not knowing why I felt that way.

My mother was never hard on me about grades, so I didn't have pressure on my back to do well. No male in the family ever finished college.

Back to school, I still remember my first day of college, how it was my way to express my intelligence. Really, I had normal knowledge. I went to college to establish a new identity. In high school I was an average guy, so going to college was my way of running to a source where I would start the next portion of my life as an adult.

I started Compton College in the fall of 2013, where I had classes with all males. My teachers were great. Being in the all-male cohort was a great experience – no female inside the classroom to cause distractions. It was an experiment the school was doing to see how well would it work to have all males in classes together with no females. Honestly, it was the best decision I made. Our teachers gave us a lot of one-on-one attention and they cared about our needs.

I made friends from all over California. Some kids went to great high schools; I became intimated because I went to my local High school and I wasn't prepared for college. I just knew I was going to finish and be the first in my family to graduate. I really excelled and developed great study habits. For first time, I went to the library and genuinely studied. I studied with others and I took pride in reading my English books.

College was my first time ever finishing reading a book. I know it may not seem like much, but for me it was big, because I had never enjoyed reading – I would just use google to cheat looking at footnotes to get a summary of each chapter. I was really putting in the work to express myself and show them that I did the reading by participating in the classroom discussions.

I also joined the football team hoping to obtain a football scholarship, but that didn't happen. One thing I take from football is character. Football helps you develop this "never quit" attitude, a character trait that I didn't have in my childhood. I was going to practice and being accountable for maintaining my grades in order to stay on the team – things that would later serve me well on a job or in business. Ever since joining, I've always had a never quit attitude.

Back to college, I had a sense of belonging, as my teacher wrote in her college dissertation. In football, you are your own man. You are accountable for your own success from fitness to being a great player. You work with others to accomplish a team goal, which can relate to the work area when you get a job working together to achieve one goal.

Playing college football, I was around grown men who weren't being forced to play; they desired as men to go out there on their own. I never quit no matter how fat I was, I just kept coming. My character was becoming better because if I could accomplish playing college ball at 5'7" playing O line, I could do anything. It gave me the confidence to want to do more. I played offensive tackle and I honestly didn't do that bad, but people were shocked to see someone so short play a position that normally someone 6'5" and above plays. My coach had faith in me and said I was a great player.

College Is where I started partying frequently; the quiet and shy boy finally got his chance to shine. When I went to parties, it was like Disneyland. I mean, seeing all the fine innocent girls shaking ass made me feel like I was in a music video. I remember my first dance. It felt like we were sexing on the floor, but we all knew I wasn't doing nothing.

My first time going to the club was with my friends from class. I was nervous and didn't know what expect. As we got in there, seeing all the fine woman blew my mind. It was like candy everywhere, girls smelling good and looking outstanding. I would get all kind of dances and my friends would just look at me and laugh. Partying became my way of finally fitting in with the crowd who I despartly admired.

My first time messing with a girl In college was awkward, because she walked up to me very aggressively. I was not used to that, so I didn't know what to do. She said, "You're handsome," and I looked at her and said, "Yeah?" You can use your imagination for what happened after that. I remember telling my friends. I was so happy, it was like I was going to them with news that I met the president. I would never forget the encounter she and I shared together.

My final semester at junior College, I was blessed to be selected to go on a Black College Tour along with other Blacks students that qualified for the trip. It was an opportunity for us to continue our schooling at an HBCU. It was my first time being on a plane, let alone having a semi-vacation away from home. It was a life-changing week that I will forever be grateful for. Our first stop was in New Orleans. We went to few colleges. They fed us and we would go to the hotel, have game night, listen to music, and have a good time. The next morning, we would load up on the bus and continue our journey throughout the south.

Our next stop was in Atlanta to visit Morehouse College and Clark. One of my favorite colleges was Morehouse, the college that Martin Luther King Jr. attended and graduated from. Just the way they dressed and carried themselves - they had the walk of success.

One moment that I would never forget was when they asked all the males how the trip impacted our lives. Honestly, the first time being a plane was something big for me. Just knowing how it feels to take off, it was unreal. I was a kid with 20 years of living in the hood and finally experience being on a plane. Most kids in the hood never get to experience that because of financial reasons. And I had the opportunity to get on a plane for free!

Meeting people from down south and seeing their mannerisms blew my mind. People answering with ma'am or sir – that was really dope. To see that made me realize the difference between us Cali folks and down south people; *big* difference! Even though I didn't transfer to an HBCU due to not having enough money, I would like to personally thank my junior College for the once in a lifetime experience. It opened doors in my mind that I didn't know were possible until being in a different environment. I graduated junior college with an AA degree in Psychology and I was on my way to finishing my 4-year degree.

I transferred to my 4 year university in fall of 2016. That was a sad moment for me because I still wanted to play football, but God's plans were different for me. Going there felt like a normal college, not in the sense of teaching, but the commuting. I had dreams of staying on campus and living on my own. I just went to school and left once my last class was over. I had one friend that I talked to and honestly, if it hadn't been for her, I probably wouldn't have even tried talking to anyone else.

I graduated in 2018 with my bachelor's degree in psychology, but something still didn't seem right. I never felt competent to be a successful man. I thought college was my way of finding myself, but I didn't.

Through social media, I was able to enhance my personality with whatever the fuck I wanted, using the way I dressed and making smart statements. I used to go to google to look up something fancy to say and put my own twist to it. Instagram is a place where you can be whoever you want to be. Hell, people don't know what's behind your screen; they see only what you allow them to see. Instagram was my way to seem cool. There are many people to look up to while surfing the web. I mentally became damaged because of the delusion of putting other people's lifestyle on mine.

Trying to be like someone else will damage the image that God already gave us. It will later destroy our true feeling of ourselves, and we almost develop a self-hate. I would also try to buy things to cover who I was, but once that high was over, I would be back to myself. This "high" that I discovered in my mid 20s was a feeling that we all experience while reaching success or discovering ourselves, but it later became my downfall.

I'll explain: First, we begin to lose sight of who we really are. Second, we begin to interact with people with a sub-conscious mind. Third, we lose ourselves in the process. My problem with social media was that it made me an imposter. I was scared to talk to women in person; when I did, it went no where.

I remember I used to write posts that made me seem cool and people a would gravitate toward me, but in my head I was still me – a nobody, a fat kid who was truly lost in his own world. When I would meet new people, I would freeze up and have bad anxiety attacks because I couldn't come up with the right words to engage in dialogue.

One evening I went to a social gathering at a little event that was held at my junior College. There was a lot beautiful lady there along with guys. As I walked in and scanned the room, I began to panic with nervousness. I could tell that people knew because I was distant and didn't give off the energy of engagement. I was always like that because social media wasn't there to fill in what I lacked as an individual. I was so embarrassed that day that I went home crying because I felt like a strange person to myself. I could not figure my own self out.

Also, when my friends and I would be together talking about relationships with woman that we liked, I would sit there and make up shit that I had no clue about. All I knew was having sex from time to time and going out to eat.

My friends would talk about how they were a "mack daddy," but I knew they were capping. Ask me how I know: I'm a Gemini, air sign. Whenever I would hear them talk, I would listen with a genuine ear. You could always tell if they were full of crap by the crack and flow of their voice.

Even my close friends never learned who I was, because I was always hiding behind mystery. I never allowed people into the circle that I created. During my time on social media, I would post statuses and pictures of myself to seem like I was engaging in life, but really, I was trying to fit in so people could look at me as somebody.

My whole life, I was quiet, sometimes friendly if you ask me. I always shut down on people when I sensed danger from them. But I opened my heart to people who I felt safe around. During my senior year of high school, my Hispanic friend and I became good friends. I never understood why I felt so comfortable with her. I enjoyed being around her, and I would always joke around.

Now, if I joke around you, then I like you. My 5'3" good friend "Vanilla". We eventually ended up at the same university where we hung out and made each day better with our laughs and good conversations. I can't remember a bad day, except when she didn't make it. When I was around her, she got the real me, not the guy I pretended to be.

I developed this shell that protected me from the bad experiences I had growing up – the teasing in school, to people not genuinely liking me for me. So, whenever I met people, I would examine everything about them before talking to them. That's why at church or school, people never really knew me like that. They only knew the big kid that played football and asked girls for sex.

Confidence, Where Are You?

I had no confidence
I lived in fear, fear of not being good enough for
anything or anyone
So God never allowed me to get what I wanted
I leaned toward the world for validation/
visibility and ended up getting my heart
crushed
That's why I always aimed so low for myself
I understand why God had to put holds on
things that I would've destroyed
I lied so much because I didn't know who I was
I pretended and pushed away people who
meant good for me
I'm here to rewrite those terrible habits,
fuck the world
I follow God's path for me
I get horny sometimes and lose focus, but I
get back to where I need to be – "reality"
I will have a beautiful Black family and lots of
laughter and joy.

No one knew my backstory. It was me putting shit on top of shit. I lost track of who I truly was as a person. My attitude changed at home, not in being disrespectful, but in the way I would carry myself. I had no true understanding of what it meant to be myself.

I thought people would catch on, because I was never really that outgoing outside of social media. I mean, I joked around of course, but when it came down to being serious, the conversation could never go very far because I wasn't that type of person. What I mean by "that type of person" is the person that everyone saw me as on social media. I think with social media, we tend to latch on to people and quotes that emotionally get us instead of working on ourselves. Don't get me wrong, on social media you can promote yourself, but we tend to move away from our true self. Social media becomes a tool that we all use to enhance who we are.

Traveling helped me grow as an individual. My thinking expanded outside of just Compton. I saw a side of the world that was different from my block and the conversation I heard at home. I remember my first trip out of the country was to Jamaica, where I saw families and couples enjoying life and creating memories together. Those were moments that I never experienced at home. Also, the genuine people I met while I was there, seeing what poor looked like – I thought skid row was bad! People were in the same condition as them, but their spirit was bright and they were very thankful people.

Seeing that, I learned the true meaning of being humble: life is precious and every day is a blessing. Seeing them being able to wake up to life and not complain because they don't have expensive "stuff" made me realize how important character is. Without character, you're no one; people don't even want to be around you, let alone support you. I remember going to clubs to see individuals enjoy each other, not wearing fancy clothes or jewelry, It was just us and the good music.

While I was in Jamaica, I met a really good guy from Washington D.C. He was about 20 years older than me. We partied almost every day of our stay, and I must admit we clicked as if we had known each other for years, I still keep in contact with him to this day. We exchanged stories of our hometown, as well our background far as what we do.

On our third day, we went on an excursion together, and while on the excursion we learned bout the history of Jamaica – how witchcraft is so big out there. They tour guide explained that a lady came from Europe and had thousands of slaves who were scared she would cast spell on them. I was really intrigued and blown away by that.

I had the opportunity to go off the resort and meet a guy's family in the mountains where there were no lights or running water to bathe in. The house looked like a shack with no windows. The house contained little to no furniture. It was surrounded by trees and fruit. It smelled so good – fruity and natural. I remember I had to use the bathroom, but their bathroom was outside. Thank goodness I didn't have to take a number two. It was like watching the Discovery Channel in rural areas, but now I was actually there.

We sat on the porch and I listened to their stories of how they survive on a day-to-day basis. One guy was 80 years old and in shape "ripped"! I was obese and felt really uncomfortable looking like that, seeing a guy 59 years older than me taking care of himself. The guy that brought me to the house had a bottle of rum liquor. At that time I wasn't big on drinking…well, I never liked drinking. I pretended I was so I engaged with drinking, but I had one cup and was done. It was good, I most confess.

In Jamaica, many don't have health care and it amazes me that they live longer and look healthier than the average American. You would think that we come from a better place and we have better resources, but you'd be wrong. They showed me the medicine that they make from different plants and how they process it naturally by having the fruit sealed in a jar for months. They were some of the healthiest people I ever met.

I spent some time on the beach with a pretty brown-skinned woman. She was from England, but she had family from Montego Bay. We talked about a lot, come to find out she was well into her 40s. From her looks, I sure couldn't tell. But hey, I was out of the country and I wanted to create as many memories as possible.

She thought I had game by the way I would smooth talk, but I was just mimicking shit I heard on the street back home. Well it worked, thanks friends. That was my first ever macking a girl down like I was Bishop Don Juan. It made me feel like the man out here getting girls on the Caribbean Island.

I can't forget to tell you about the beautiful ladies I encountered during my stay. They were genuinely nice and their bodies were from a another world! I mean, thick lips and the clearest skin you would ever want to see! And the way they moved at the parties was like none other. I thought they were casting a spell on me the way I couldn't stop staring, and their gorgeous accent had my "ting" going crazy.

During that trip I learned what true love was. At home, I thought having nice shoes and clothes made you attractive, but our character overrides all that. It's the way we make people feel when we meet them. Those material things don't really mean anything. Who are we once the material things come off? Do we still feel valuable? Do we still treat others with respect?

These are things we don't talk about; it's not about what we have to have in order for people to like us. True living is how you impact other people's lives; the more you pour into others, the more God pours into your life. I noticed when I was being stingy, the weight I packed on and I could never figure out why. But once I became more giving, God began to open up doors.

In 2018 I decided to go to Europe for college graduation gift. How excited I was to go, honestly, I was more excited about trying the sweets then the seeing the Eiffel Tower "just kidding". I became interested in going to Europe because I wanted to learn about European history and their psychology. I learned Western psychology, I just wanted to further my studies.

When I was in Europe being around the Eiffel Tower and seeing a lot of poor white people made me realize that Black people are not the only ones struggling in the world. I thought whites were all doing well. Never did I ever see whites struggle before until I went to Paris. I was 23 years old, and honestly, my visit to Paris was a great eye opener. Not in the sense of being better than them, but in seeing how people everywhere share the same struggle. Also, seeing my beautiful Black people out there made me feel welcomed; meeting Blacks from all over the world was amazing to me.

The fashion was dope out there – I mean there was nothing like it. But more than the superficial things, while in Europe I saw a lot of Black history. Not to dig deep, but Black history goes back thousands of years years. It was also nice seeing Black art inside the subways. I did not experience any racism out there! People were looking at me more as if I were a celebrity because I was from the famous city "Compton, California." I was like a lost child filled with nothing but nostalgic moments.

While on the trip, I stumbled across a young lady from Philly. She was about 5'4" with brown skin and a pretty smile. Her hotel was by mine and when I saw her standing outside, a brother couldn't resist introducing himself. For some reason, I was not shy or hesitant to talk to her. Hell, I thought she wouldn't even speak to me, but she was happy when I approached and talked to her.

By the second day, we deciding to roam the city and continue sight-seeing. As we went to the city, she had another friend from Thailand who was extremely nice as well. She took us to see all kinds of sights, and she treated us to a Nutella waffle. I enjoyed the Nutella; I felt like a kid again.

My new Philly friend and I went to Notre Dame church where we talked about Black history as well as world history. It was like a great connection; I felt really good being with her. After that we went back to our hotels and exchanged numbers. We became really good friend long distance.

Before leaving Paris, I took a trip to Disney Paris and I must confess it was like being on another world. I been to Disneyland here in Cali, but going in another country – yeah, that was big. I quickly noticed how fit everyone was, and how big I was compared to the average guy there. That was why people were staring at me. I remember I bought a 2 XL shirt and it felt like a medium shirt. I guess clothes are made different over there.

What I took from that trip was the experience of many different walks of life from a different perspective. Seeing whites from different parts of the world and also seeing my people was a great experience. Oh yeah, to Paris - your women were outstanding and gorgeous! I thought L.A. and New York had the beauty, but nothing like the pretty women in Paris. To the sister from Philly that I met during my short stay was fun and had a pleasant vibe.

Moving on to Dubai, Dubai was an awesome trip. My whole trip was less than $900. Let me tell you how God works! Going to Dubai was a total shocker! Never once would I have ever imagined seeing so much money and how people acted with wealth, acted normal versus how people with money in the U.S. acted. It was totally different outlook

I was used to how people here in the U.S. treat people when they have money – how their attitude changes toward people, and how they create distance between themselves and people who have less. I think it's a form of low self-esteem. Why get money just to stunt on people you've known for a lifetime? People in Dubai were super nice. You couldn't really tell who had the most money, because they all acted the same.

During my short stay there, I met a couple from Atlanta, Georgia. They were really nice; we met when I went camel riding. They were married with three children, I believe. We were talking and they began to ask me questions like, "Who did you come with?" I told them I came by myself. They asked, "What you do," and I said I work for Ralph's grocery market and I'm a football coach. I explained to them that I travel every year, I take a vacation to somewhere that's different from where I stay. Further explaining I travel because it helps me gain more knowledge of myself and also learn about the world. I told them I'm from Compton and of course their eyes lit up like they'd hit a lottery number.

I once thought having money, you had to show people you got it, but that was a terrible mindset. People in Dubai had money but lived so freely and honestly. They didn't dress fancy or anything, they were just being themselves on God's green land. What an amazing experience, and to that girl that I met in the elevator, you were no joke – and I mean that with a passion! I love women from all walks of life, and she was definitely in the top 5 in my book.

September 10, 2020, at 10 a.m.

I found a job working for a warehouse in Torrance, California. There, I met this guy better known as "OG", a cool brother. Meeting him, I learned what being a man meant, from being able to take care of a family and how to emotionally take care of a wife. Honestly, out of the 25 years of my life, I never knew that, because I saw my uncles living with someone or living with a woman who had most of the responsibility.

OG was Muslim. Now I'm no Muslim, but every time we talked, it was never about nonsense. I was able to expose my flaws and the ideology that had been embedded in my head since my early teenage years. If you don't have anyone around to teach you these things, then you will grow up with a twisted mind and essentially you will live a confused life, because the world always has the answer, "so they say."

I always thought money was the answer to my problem until the money was gone and the problems were still there. Watching music videos, you begin to believe money is what makes people happy. But the videos only show what they want to sell you. No offense to Cardi B – her Lyrics are nice, but her husband still cheated on her. You begin to wonder, how can a perfect girl get cheated on when she is beautiful and has a nice body?

No matter how much money you have, no one can give you character. Because many situations will occur, but you always stay in character. I remember when I first started the job, we were working 12 hour shifts and I would bitch and complain, while millions were out of work due to COVID. OG saw me bitching and he asked me, "Do you pay rent?" and my response was, "yes." He asked, "Do you pay all of the rent on your own?" and I looked at him and said, "No."

I wanted to get offended, but I couldn't, because I didn't pay rent on my own. I mean, I gave my mom money, but that's nothing to brag about. Here I was chasing after girls like I was able to take care of them. All I was doing was getting ready to repeat the same cycle of not being competent in taking care of a family.

Men are leaders. Without a strong foundation in the house, the respect for men goes down. There are no books that say women are to provide and do everything. It's our job as men to not just fuck and have babies, but to be responsible for your actions. After our conversation, I was able to let that talk marinate and I quickly realized it was God's protection – protection from md getting into something I wasn't prepared for.

Being around OG, I first learned what it takes to be a man, not living at home with moms or trying to chase woman around to brag to friends that I fucked her and left her emotionally dry. That was the mindset of a little boy. That was why when I met a good woman, it never lasted, because the bitch was in me. Lord, I thank God for "OG."

Chasing Money

-The more I chased you, the more unhappy I got
-I want you, but I need peace
-You're not my everything
-My character speaks for me
-My smile, personality, and sense of humor
-I wish you weren't' everybody's focus
-You are either a bitch or you're not
-I'd rather bathe in love than chase something
*   that's never ending*

Money was my way of making me think I was cool, but people don't see real money. When I was working my job at the grocery market, my mother wasn't asking for much for rent, so each week I had money to play with. Here I am worshiping money, but I didn't like myself, because once my little check ran out I was back to being a nobody. I saw my friends flash money on the "gram" and it made me want to do it because of the likes and girls they would get. But I never stopped to ask how they felt inside. My personality was overridden by others.

In the ghetto, we use money to cover up our lack of self-esteem. What a sucker was I letting that mindset get to me, wanting to change for punk-ass people who didn't even know who they were. At the age of 19, I started my real job working at Ralph's grocery market. Every time I got paid, I'd run straight to mall for clothes, shoes, and other accessories to cover my scars. That got me into credit card debt.

Also, as I chased buying things, I created distance around the sweet guy that everyone seemed to love, the guy who would cook and post on Instagram and Facebook. Those were the moments that made me happy, not running to the mall chasing a one-day high for people to like me for the moment.

Money can't buy a better relationship with your parents and damn sure cannot buy back time missed from your childhood. I believe many want to talk about this. If you have so much money, then why do you have to always work to make people believe you got it? Get your family and build, because no one gives a damn about you.

I looked to money only to lose myself and lose people who were really meant to be in my life. If a person doesn't want to be in your life, believe them and move on, because there is always something that someone can take from you, and that's your peace of mind.

3

LOWEST COMMON DENOMINATOR

Eleventh grade was my first time going after a girl that I semi liked on a serious level. She was 5'0", brown skinned mixed. I can't lie, at that time she was the best thing I had ever seen. I must admit going after her made me feel good, even though she didn't like me the way I liked her. At that time, I didn't know any better and I thought it couldn't get any better. It didn't bother me when she would shoot me down. The old feeling of the way my dad would deal with me, picking me when he felt like it, getting shot down had become normal to me. I had grown accustomed to accepting when a person I was dealing with was not genuinely interested. Only seeing my dad five times a year was my happiest moments, because he allowed me to be a part of his life.

I would hang out with this girl and every time she would be nice, I would take it to the extreme and act like she really liked me. Ha! One time we went out to eat and as we sat and talked, she brought up another guy and you should've seen the look on my face – the look of a dumbass. I was so in love with this girl that I was blinded by the truth: she didn't like me. Hell, I didn't like myself, so any little thing that made me feel good or feed my ego, I would run with it. This went on for about four years, until I came to realization that I would not get her. Also seeing the men in my family dealing with the women also played a role in how I thought a relationship should be like – women dealing with men only when they felt like it.

Never quite understood why we associate ourselves with people who don't share our same mindset and are not goal oriented as we are. Now that I'm older, I realize that no matter what kind of degree or career we have, mental illness affects everyone. Starting with my family, I saw women working taking care of men.

I feel as if God sent people to show me the life that I didn't know I had. People would always talk highly about me, but they said things that I didn't see in myself. At the age of 21, a friend and I went to a club in downtown L.A., and the guys that were there had jewelry and fancy clothes. I had a on 20 dollar outfit with a fresh fade.

anyways I had a few drinks, so I wasn't consciously thinking straight. I pumped into this girl very hard nearly knocking her down to floor. She immediately got in my face in said, "Damn, you tried to knock me over!" I stayed in her face and said, "No, but you look good…" Honestly, she was probably surprised that a big square dude stood his ground, and she liked it.

I later went to my group of friends and she went with hers. We made eye contact and she gave me the sexual seduction face as we continued to stare. She made the first move and walked back up to me and asked me, "Do you see something you want?" I froze and said something corny. In my head, I was foaming at the mouth because of things I wanted to do to her, but I messed up with my scary ass. Even the guys who were dressed up were looking like what the hell was going on. I believe that night God sent that message to remind me who I was, but I couldn't hear him yet. Lord, if she only knew.

My mom's friends and cousin took care of the man and it made me sick to my stomach. I called that the single mother effect. Men tend to live with their mothers and seeing them pay the bills, men tend to take on a female role of wanting to be taking care of. When the father is not in the house, you don't see how things are supposed to be run properly and in order.

Easy as it may seem, I didn't learn about a man's responsibilities until my mid-20s. Once I graduated college, I would try to date and I even told a girl I wanted a baby. My dumb ass with no work ethic.

Hell, I didn't even like working like that. I worked part-time for Ralph's and honeslty, I hated working long shifts. I was cool working just 20 hours a week. A grown ass man with that kid mentality.

Not having a dad or seeing men work had me in delusional state of mind. I'm glad I didn't have a baby I would have ruined that kid's life as well as the mother's life. I was not a man; I was just mimicking what I saw and thought it was cool. Every time I would try to talk to a woman, I never felt right – not in a homosexual way, but I knew I wasn't a man mentally. I would go to clubs because of my friends, but I knew my life was shit and I knew I needed a change.

Physical fitness was big in my family. We were a large family and I don't mean large in numbers, but in weight. So, it was easy for me to not take P.E. in school seriously. I thought Black people was just big and we didn't need to exercise. Wrong! My health was so bad that my doctor wanted to see me twice a year and she always said, "You know you can die of a heart attack." I didn't believe her because to my knowledge no one in my family had a disease.

Comparing myself to the people of my family overrode what was important, which is health. Lack of health can limit you. I used to think I could walk around in the world big and my life wouldn't have any problem. Yeah, I had low confidence; I didn't like myself in spite of being in denial about losing weight.

Raising a child in a toxic environment can affect him or her; children will not have a foundation on how to be a man or woman while growing up. For example, I have seen women argue about how they want good men, but choose to go after men who don't even work or do not try to make an effort to work. By examining that, I came to the conclusion that we tend to gravitate toward what mentally stimulates our minds. Some people don't think highly of themselves, so they run to the person who balances out their thinking.

I say this again: career and degree don't mean anything if your mind is stuck in a place where subconsciously thinking less of yourself is part of who you are. I gravitated toward men that looked like they had it, but still had an empty soul like mine. I wanted to mimic friends at school who would dress a certain way and had jewelry, but I didn't know their story behind the person they were betraying. For some reason, I always went toward people who thought like myself. For example, when I used to go to school, pretty girls would always try to talk to me, but I didn't think I could get them, so I went toward women who had low self-esteem like myself.

I never told anyone this, but when I was in the 9th grade I wrote down a plan for what I was going to do after high school. I wrote that I wanted to get on Social Security and not have to work. That was my mentality at 14 years old. I was out of shape like all the men in my family, so I enjoyed being big and eating Hostess cupcakes and donuts. .From the age of 7 until adulthood, eating has been a big part of my life. I mean, if I wasn't eating, I was thinking about what I wanted to eat.

Our mind matches with everything that we involve ourselves with and it goes after what the mind attracts. When a woman or man wants to talk to someone, they instantly see how that person's mind is by the conversation. If they like how the person thinks, they will connect. Just look at how fast they conform to the world. Someone sets a trend – watch everyone follows. What I learned is, if we don't have control of our emotions, our minds tend to fall for anything because of the way it makes us feel instead of it being what we really want. No friend, family, or the world can give you what your heart truly desires. Many of us become unhappy because something we thought we wanted did not make us happy even though the world said it would make us feel good. Taking time out to learn your wants and needs, you understand what makes you happy when the world seems to disagree. It's important that we use what God naturally gave us, and that's integrity.

As mentioned earlier, when we conform to the world we miss out on our true selves, liking what others like and not what you like. Don't miss out on your blessing living someone else's life. This is prevalent today because many of us fall short of what it's really meant for us to have in this world because our thinking is low. Our family standards have made a heavy impression on our own mind, and we are scared to leave those standards to try something that we've never seen before.

I never imagined that my mind would deteriorate from wanting the complete opposite of what I saw growing up. We see trauma in our family, but go out to recreate the situation with someone else.

I began to go toward women that the men in my family were attracted to. It's funny, because every time I would meet that type of woman, I would always feel like I wasn't supposed to be there. But mentally my mind was in like a prison of not wanting to leave. Psychologically my mind was fucked. I never told anyone, I just acted like everything was fine because that was what I was used to seeing. Growing up In the ghetto, all that I seen was low income and fathers not being competent taking care of their family. The pattern I have detected in my family is low self-esteem, from the way we carry ourselves to the relationships we get into. It hurts my heart knowing how beautiful we are, but our minds are so low that we fall for anything.

Love is not hard to find when integrity and attention are real. Everything starts in our mind. If we have negative thoughts before something happens, we tend to go into any situation with a horrible mindset. For example, I would struggle with a woman because my mind would already be defeated. The woman would gravitate toward me, but my mind was just in the dugout, scared to come out.

I must confess that early on in my years, I developed some toxic traits that played a role in my personality. I thought having a degree and career would make me a great guy. Boy, was I wrong. I was a scared boy, running around with this fake personality that led to me chasing after people who had the same thinking as I had. I would pretend everything was okay when it wasn't.

I noticed in the type of women I attracted, how they were just as dumb as I was. Pretty as they were, our mind had a big disease in it. I came today to rectify that problem and kill the low thinking. I never understood the price of integrity until I met people and events that exposed the terrible lying monster inside me. I was so afraid of a certain woman because I knew I wasn't shit as a person; honestly, I needed that.

4

FAKE PERSONALITY

Timing

Timing is what created distance between us
Timing had me pretending
Timing made me rush into something I wasn't ready for
Timing exposed the boy in me
Timing is the reason you came back only to discover
I still wasn't ready
Now, I wait till my time, not the world's time

Hello, pussy, the man that pretended for years. Yeah, I'm talking about myself. Here I stand for the first time in my life and tell you that I'm done running from the man in the mirror, the guy who loves to cook and make people laugh. I mean, that's why so many people loved me at school. I do not wish to walk one more step without walking in integrity. I, Brent Palmer, would like to punch the old me in the gut and rectify my lies and image. I never knew what self-love was. I just knew that satisfying the world and making them accept me would make me feel good, so I pretended and I hurt some people who didn't need to be hurt. Also, I led friends and potential partners with this fake image. Here I come today as Brent "Donquise" Palmer, the "quiet boy" who loves poems and writing.

I never told anyone that I like poems, because I didn't want to come off as soft. I guess the weight of acceptance was my main focus. I used to brag to my friends about pulling girls left to right, but in reality I just fronting. I acted like I was so intelligent in school, but I was doing the bare minimum to get by.

In 2009, I entered high school with no idea of what I would become. I was just an overweight kid coming from middle school with little to no confidence in myself. Joining football was my only means of recreating my image and making people think differently about me. My main focus was to change the narrative about me: momma's boy, kid that ate for fun, and the kid who thought low of himself.

On May 12, 2009, at around 3:30 p.m., I walked onto to the Compton High football field at 315 pounds, and immediately saw that there were drills set out with a lot of cardio involved. In my head, I was asking myself how in the hell I was going to get through that as easy as possible. I didn't like to hurt, because hurting was punishment for me and I didn't like the feeling. I was nervous, but everybody welcomed me with open arms.

The first day, one of the line coaches liked me because of my size and wanted to work with me. Coach even gave me a nickname "ham hock" and all my teammates starting laughing. All I could remember was laughing and watching the cheerleaders practice. I had a friend from middle school on the cheer team. We had known each other since elementary school and her grandmother was my daycare lady. I had a little crush on her, but I was too scared to press her, so I left her alone.

The head coach was our leader. He had a great staff that stressed hard work. They would baby me because I was out of shape and they didn't want me to quit, so I didn't have to deal with being pushed hard. I had no idea what hard work was, I just knew saying hard work would make me feel good about myself.

Entering high school had goals that I had to obtain. Those goals consist of being popluar and getting with as many cheerleaders as possible. Seeing the cheerleaders in booty shorts and tank tops, my little man was going crazy. Everybody thought I was nice guy, which I was, but they didn't know what was going on in my head. My attitude changed; I wanted to be more like my teammates who were getting vagina and love. That was the type of intimacy that I desperately wanted. I never knew what love was, I just knew it would make me feel like a man.

When you think of a person having a fake personality, you think of someone who is not being true to himself. I was struggling with myself. Deep down, I developed this strong negative attitude about myself, because I didn't know who I was. I didn't take the time to learn and appreciate who Brent Palmer was. Never could I wrap my head around it; however, I tried to maintain an image of being this perfect guy, so I could be liked at school and try to impress girls.

One of the more interesting things I can tell you is that many girls were interested in me, but I just never believed it. Around my 11th grade year, a young woman walked up to me after school and called me handsome. Honeslty, I damn near shitted on myself because I couldn't believe a woman that fine would say that to me. We later connected on Instagram. She would comment on my pictures and I still couldn't believe it.

Man, if only she knew how bad I wanted her, but I didn't have the skills and knowledge on how to get her. Those interactions lasted for about a couple of months, but after she discovered there was no alpha in me, she went on to the guy who was ready to receive her. I never told her this, but she made me feel good about myself when she would give me compliments. I would walk around school and my friends would ask me, "Who was that commenting on your picture?" I'd play like I didn't know who they were talking about.

Part of the distance between women and me came from my being overweight; psychologically it messed with my brain. Due to me not being myself, I knew a woman would pick up on it. I have a saying, "Fellas, women know when you are not acting like your true character."

I would hide from girls and not show affection toward them, to the point that some of my friend thought maybe I was gay. Even my mom once asked me about my manhood, because this girl at my church liked me but I didn't like her back.

Honestly, I always knew what I liked in a woman, just never went after what I really wanted because of the fear of rejection. I rejected myself far more times than anyone else could have. So, going into interacting, I would play a scenario in my head with a chick turning me down.

I wanted to be like my fit friends so bad that I started to act like them, but with a bigger and nastier body. I would talk to the girls the way my friends would – with a whisper in their ear.

I once told a girl I could make her vagina wet. Shit, the only thing I could make wet at that time was her eyes with my funny jokes. The woman knew I was a bitch but they accepted it, until they went with who they really wanted.

When it came to academics, I was a fair kid – below average, but I was still able to maintain grades that got me by just enough to be able to play football and graduate on time. My moms wasn't really tripping on a high GPA, so doing the bare minimum to pass was cool with her. I later found out what you put in is what you get.

Growing up, I struggled with academics, mostly English. I learned that English has been a problem within my family for years, so I guess it continued on to me. I never told anyone, but when we would be in school, I would hate to read out loud. Not because I couldn't read, but because I wasn't at the reading level I should've been. My mother tried to get me help with it, but I never took it seriously. I guess the motivation and the need to learn wasn't there for me.

Since kindergarten, from what I can remember, my academics were very poor. My kindergarten teacher told my mom that I was struggling with comprehending and recommended that I take medicine to focus.

One morning my teacher called my mother out of the blue and she had her stand in back without me noticing. When I found out she was behind me, I was nervous and I couldn't do anything but act right.

She pulled me outside the door and talked to my mother and had some suggestions for me that would be beneficial in her eyes, but my mother refuse to put me on the pills. At that time, Black children were being targeted heavily into taking medicine "to focus." I guess it was a social experiment that schools wanted to try on kids in the ghetto. From kindergarten to 12th,grade I would remain average.

To combat my incompetence in English literature, I would talk smart around people. In reality we were on the same playing field, same level of learning ability. If the school had put me with the failing students, we would have been just as smart as each other. However, I excelled in math and science. When I took science seriously, I became very proficient at it. I knew I wasn't the fittest, nor the most handsome at school, so I had to be good at something. The whole idea was to "fake it until you make it."

Yeah, fellas don't believe that façade, because sooner or later those things that you claim you're good at will catch up to you and you will have to prove it. In eleventh grade, I signed up for honors English, where I failed miserably. My 11th grade teacher knew I was a dumb ass, sitting in there like I belonged.

Honestly, I was living a lie, knowing I should be in a remedial class to get help with the basics of English. That was a time I'll never forget.

I knew I had problems learning, but I was too much of a pussy to admit it and get help.

One moment I remember is when we had do a presentation and when I went up there, I totally froze, not knowing where to start or how to conduct myself. I'm glad I put myself in that position, because I wanted to break a shell that I never told anyone about. I honestly signed up for it in the sense of crying for help, because I wasn't getting the push at home that I would have liked. As long as I passed, my mother stayed off my back, so there was no pressure to go beyond what I had been doing.

Even my 12th grade year wasn't great; still the same results from my 11th grade year. Luckily, I passed and moved on to junior college. I remember applying and taking the placement test to see where I was. Lord Jesus, if you saw my result, you'd think I learned under a rock. I scored so low, I thought I would graduate junior college in four years, because I had to take so many remediation classes to come up to speed with English.

Luckily, I was invited to join the all-male cohort class where they had accelerated classes to finish faster. I struggled in the beginning, but eventually got help and did fairly well. All through college, when I had to do presentations I would freeze up and stutter. It came from knowing I didn't belong there with students who were far ahead of me. I don't see how I didn't quit. I was just a big-time disaster. But through the embarrassment, I continued and it made me stronger.

For the first time, my dumb ass will admit I graduated college being mediocre. I graduated, but still felt like I accomplished nothing. All the time, I never studied and barely got by, but what you take for granted will come back to haunt you. It was hard for me to admit that, because as a Black male, you want to show the world that you are able to comprehend and excel.

I could blame the hood schools I attended, but only we know what we have to work on. I'm glad I can finally admit that. Faking like I was smart was my insecurity of owning up to struggling. I believe that most kids act up in school because they don't know how to learn, so they use that eccentric behavior to cover up their incompetence.

Other acts that made me a joke were me going out to clubs and later posting pictures on Instagram to make it seem like Brent Palmer was the man. When I would go clubbing, I would dance and talk to girls, but women were dancing with me subconsciously because liquor. Ha! Or maybe they genuinely wanted to dance; in any case, I would end up taking the dance floor.

That was my only claim to fame –having people think I had all the girls. Honestly, I was the guy with the lowest self-esteem in the club trying to look cool. I can't make this up, but women would always stare at me in the club and I always wondered what they were thinking. With my self-esteem so low, I thought it was bad.

That's the life I was living in my head. When leaving the club and going home, the emptiness would take over my body, because the high was over and it was back to reality. I was a man with low self-esteem that couldn't stand himself at times.

Do I blame my dad, or take the blame myself? I, Brent Palmer, take the blame because we all know who we are; we either choose to accept or try to be something that we're not. I struggled with girls, not because I couldn't get one, but because my image of myself was so low that I needed to be something or have something material to cover up my insecurity. It was so bad that my health began to decline. I would eat until it felt like I was going to pass out. That was the only time I felt happiness within myself. Reading this, you see the mental illness that was formed in my head. That made me subconsciously approach every situation with unrealistic thinking.

Things

> *-What would you be if you didn't have things*
>   *that made you stand out?*
> *-Would you still approach shorty?*
> *-If you didn't wear a chain and a designer outfit*
>   *would you still feel accomplished?*
> *-If you didn't have that designer bag*
>   *to compliment your hard work, would you*
>   *still feel like accomplished 'ladies"?*
> *-Fellas, if you were stripped of all your fancy cars would you still*
>   *feel proud of the man you are?*
> *-Girls, would you still feel beautiful if that ass wasn't fat?*
> *-Who are we without those things? Do you live for approval,*
>   *or for genuine love?*
> *-I love me, 5'7" and all: great looking, great personality, God fearing,*
>   *funny, great lover*
> *"Quality over quantity" – that's what I told Bruh!*

In early spring of 2014, I met this girl woman through a mutal. She went to a school that was approximately 10 minutes away from my high school. It all started with a status that I posted, which she commented on it and I had the courage to message with the intent of getting to know her. It was small talk at first; it took a while to get the number. We continued our communication through Facebook for about a month until finally she gave me her number.

We talked, and honestly, I didn't know what the hell to talk about, but we were talking. What made me like her was her posts; I could relate to them and I felt them on a deep level. She was shaped the way I liked it, dark-skinned and gorgeous. We had a long talk on the phone once; it went for almost an hour. I don't know how It lasted, but It dld.

My inexperience with dating – well, before we go on, I want you to close your eyes and imagine seeing everything that you prayed for finally come true. I don't want to say her name; we'll call her "Chocolate." This is one of the most nostalgic moments, but the learning lesson that happened in my life would be my first real date. I remember meeting her at the restaurant for the first time, this beautiful chocolate girl that I connected with through a mutual friend.

Honestly, she was so gorgeous and I couldn't believe she would even give me a chance, but luckily we ended up talking for some months. I would schedule dates, but somehow my schedule would get in the way, until one day we finally went on our first date together at Olive Garden.

That was my first real date with someone that I saw myself being with. When we met, walking up to meet her for the first time, my heart was pounding and I was very nervous.

I remember the date like it was yesterday. Walking up to her for the first time was like meeting one of your favorite celebrities; it was just breathtaking. It was awkward, because there was no internet and no post to make me seem like an awesome guy. Not saying I'm not an awesome guy, but it was like the Super Bowl for me to show her what I was made of.

I guess reality hit when I heard her gorgeous voice. My heart started to pound, and my nervousness took over. I was nervous because I knew that I didn't deserve her, and I also knew that I had no idea how to be in a relationship.

She wasn't like any other woman that I tried to get with; she was the real deal "my thinking at the time, HA". This is a moment that I will never forget. I was exposed in a big way, leading this person on like I was this "player." If only she knew – which she did.

I'll never forget Virgo! Even though it wasn't a success, I learned a valuable lesson. I learned how integrity plays a big role in who you are as a person. After the date, we would talk every now and then, and I believe we would have met again, but I still had trouble being myself. Honestly, it was the fact that I knew I didn't know what to do as a man.

While we were talking, I could never open up her to her. I can't explain why I had trust issues with her. With any other girl, I could easily open and talk about anything. I had girls that I played around with, but this girl was someone I could see myself building a family, love, and life with. Again, "my thinking at the time"

These are things that I wanted, but I didn't have the foundation on how to make it happen. I can only imagine how things could've been, but these are lessons that we as men have to learn, man up, and do better. I don't take it as a failure, more of a reality check.

My meeting with a woman with the same common denominator finally came to end. I always felt comfortable around women who I shared the same mental thinking with, but with her, sir, it was a no-go.

I can honestly say how much I appreciate her in a big way. Not because we went on a date, but because meeting her helped me expose my weakness, and I personally would like to thank her for that. I thought she was weird, but how could she be when I was the real weirdo?

Also, my conscience always bothers me when I know I'm not worthy of something, and I knew I wasn't right for her at that time. Sometimes we meet people at the wrong time, but in life you move on to something better or that's really meant for you. At that time that's how I thought, however, if had a role model that wouldve never happen with me being desperate over someone. Never would I allow my kids to think so low of themselves.

"What God Sees"

Maybe what I see is a blank bliss,
*   from being weak, and my lack in God.*
As I look back on my life, I see why I didn't
*   end up with certain situations.*
I know I wasn't in shape mentally or physically
*   for anyone.*
But what I see now, I thank God for saving me
From the disaster;
*   it would've been a repeat of the family cycle.*
Or maybe God seen my inmaturness in my incompetencey.

I'm not trying to understand God's plan;
instead, I seek his plan through discipline.
By doing the right thing he will reveal his plan,
but I have to have integrity.
I guess I need to loosen up and start thinking
highly about myself: handsome, educated,
funny, and hardworking.

God doesn't give you anything when you are mentally defeated; that's why we don't get certain things. When I was immature, I use to get mad, but now I see why God will hold things until you're mentally ready.

I had this big problem, going around asking girls for sex. I will never forget my freshman year of high school. My mother signed me up for a summer job where I started working for a restaurant. There, I met this girl who I would ask for sexual favors. Now I was only 13 or 14 at the time. I would subconsciously be going around looking for sex. I was at work on a hot summer day and this girl gave me her number, and me thinking with the little head, I started talking dirty. She gave me a little sexual talk back, but I took it to the extreme.

I remember she told the boss and instead of him disciplining me, he just simply talked and told me that what I was doing wasn't right and he knew I didn't know any better. I later apologized and went on with my summer job. I was socially awkward for after that, because I had to look them in the face every day for the remainder of the summer job. I moved on and continued after, but in a calmer way. I was just a horny, porn watching little boy.

It's crazy how the older I get, the more I realize how stupid that was. But honestly, boys will do that because of their curiosity and wanting to fit with peers. Also, I was watching porn. I'll never forget I got caught watching porn when I was about 7 or nine. I found my mom's porn tapes and she busted me watching. After that, I started watching porn via phone internet. Looking at that at that age, you discover what the thing between your legs can do and it builds up this energy that is uncontrollable. However, those images playing in my head had me wanting to do the nasty every day, which later led to me doing weird behavior at school.

It's crazy how it can twist your mind up and have your penis throbbing. I can honestly say I didn't know what I was doing, I just knew it fired me up. So, I would go to school with the image in my head and ask girls for those types of sexual favors. My early years of high school, I wasn't sexually active. The most I ever did was feel booty and kiss a girl on the cheek. I would get around friends and pretend like I was experiencing getting some pussy. I knew I was lying, but it felt good to be a part of that conversation.

Honestly, I didn't start getting sexually active until I was 17. I guess the porn would really have me thinking about it a lot. The first time that I jacked off was at the age of 12 or 13, I believe. I remember I busted a nut and after that fantastic moment was over, the "white stuff" would come out. I didn't know what was coming out of my penis. I didn't tell my mom, so I went to the internet and learned what happens when men reach that point of climax. These are areas that I learned on my own. I would say to children around the world if you have questions about sex, please don't hesitate to ask questions. My thinking was beyond immature.

These are the events that made up this imposter of a person that I proclaim was perfect. I knew it would eventually catch up to me, and I worked hard on keeping up the image of this great individual. One thing that I take from all the fraud that was created by me is I can finally admit to my wrongs and fix whatever issue I had with myself before meeting someone else.

Part of my insecurity comes from having a terrible relationship with my mom. If you have a bad relationship with your mom, then more than likely you will have a bad one with a partner. Now, I see why my previous engagement with a woman was a struggle. Once you begin to fix the relationship with your mother, you will begin to have a better relationship with women. I would try to talk to a girl, but come home with hate and malice toward the Queen that birthed me. Partially, I can say it comes from my mom and dad's relationship. My mom would bring his name up if she was going to pick up child support, or she would bash his name and call him names that were not appropriate.

Parents if you're reading this, understand that your relationship with your kids can really affect their way of thinking once they part ways from you. If you don't teach them, then the world will begin to indoctrinate their minds with beliefs that are not always true.

Love

-I thought I could buy you.
-Even thougth I can dress you.
-Hell, even thougth I can pretend.
-But true love is not expressed through our image.
-It's the deep connection we get from each other.
-I guess the "high" of having things had me blind
    from what was important
-I thought love was about penetrating you
    and not caring for you after.
-You put your clothes back on, and the feeling
    I had before we did it was gone, like that: nut.
-I couldn't even look you in your eyes
-I didn't see myself with you, neither did I
    want to start a family with you
-That's the coward in me, if I acknowledge that.
-Love is something beyond sex; it's loving you
    before dessert.
-How I hold you and we lay side by side
    and shower with genuine purpose.
-Will love ever be this simple?

by Brent Palmer

5

LAW ENFORCEMENT

Timing

-Timing is what created distance between us
-Timing exposed the boy in me
-Timing is the reason I failed, because
I wasn't ready
-Timing prepared me for Greater
-You're the reason I'm in shape
-You're the reason for great penmanship
-You're the reason for God's purpose
-You're the reason for overflow
-Thank you: timing

In late march of 2019 at 10:30 p.m., I found myself sitting in the dark crying after coming back from my vacation from dubai. Now you would think I'd be well rested and happy, but on this particular night, a sad cloud came over me. I wasn't happy with the current Job I was at; it made me very frustrated when I knew I had to go to work. So, I turned on my computer and was scrolling through jobs when the police department popped up with an entry level test date and location. I hesitated at first, because where I'm from cops are hated. Hell, I live in the city that made the song about "F*ck the Police." If you asked any kid in elementary school what they wanted to be, the typical answer would be firefighter or policeman, but I never seriously thought about joining.

I signed up, passed the test at the adult school, and started my long process for the police Academy. At that time, I was 290 or more; looking across the room, the other guys were really small. I remember thinking there was no way an hell I would ever get down to their sizes, because being in shape had never crossed my mind. I was into weightlifting, so if you got me under that bench, I'd show you some real competition, Ha.

Once I you passed the entry level test, I you start with the process. During the process, you're highly encouraged to join the CAP program that gets you ready for the Academy. But I was so scared because I had never ran long distance or exercised to get in good shape. I was always comfortable being average and not excelling.

I remember one of the sergeants was shopping where I worked the grocery and I stopped her to ask about the process. She looked at me with a serious demeanor and I told her I was in the process of joining the the police department. She looked at me and said, "You need to lose weight." Now, I never heard someone tell me that before, until I meet her, however, it was neccesary. I mean I heard my coaches and doctors tell me that me, but her tone of voice was for real and she meant well!

All my life people in my family had been telling me I was cute and girls like chubby dudes. Whether that true or not, how far is it going to take you in life? I became an overweight adult with no goals or ambition whatsoever. Once the sergeant purchased her groceries, she gave me some tips on how to eat healthy. I acted like I was engaged, but in my head I was going to get a honey bun to satisfied my craving. I had no clue about healthy eating. I would still buy processed food and eat canned vegetables. She gave me her business card and before long I lost it.

I wasn't serious. Hell, I didn't think I would follow through with the process. I would look at videos of the police Academy training and become very discouraged. My problem was, I couldn't see myself in shape with a badass body that looked like I could tear some stuff up.

Months went by, and I finally decided to go to one of the workouts that was offered in Inglewood, California, about 15 minutes away from Compton. Walking out to the track and seeing candidates thin and in shape was new to me. I was used to the hood sports team: eating bad, playing like shit.

This was new to me; it was like walking into a new world. I felt uncomfortable because I had never been around people of that caliber. Our first run was about three miles. I struggled big time, and my push-ups and sit-ups were horrible. I couldn't even get over the wall because my upper body was terrible. After that, I stop going for a while. I was too embarrassed that I didn't have what it took to be there. Can't lie, I got a little discouraged, but God didn't let me quit. He saw something in me that I didn't see.

Purpose

Turning the tables around for my health,
 relationships and learning ability
I have the chance to end that with me
No more playing myself, not in the sense of
wanting material things or a relationship,
But turning my life to where it was destined to be
Being lazy got me nowhere; not taking school
 seriously troubled me
Now I'm paying for it
All the times I chased pussy, I was actually
 the pussy
This is my moment to change the family pattern forever

Thank God for diggin' in that ass. I needed that.

I continued my long process while still working part time at Ralph's. When I got close to finishing the process, I began to go to the CAP program more often. I eventually got a little better, but there was not too much improvement. Then COVID hit and classes were shut down. I'll remind you that I was already lazy, so I definitely had trouble doing the workouts on my own. I would still eat as if I could afford to eat bad.

I continued with my family tradition of doing the same old thing: being lazy with the victim mindset, like people are just going to hand you a medal when you didn't do the work. Receiving government aid and Section 8 had me content and comfortable because every month I knew my mom's rent would be paid and I'd go eat a burger and fries and go to a party with hopes of finding a woman to be my better half. In reality, I wasn't good for myself.

My sources of inspiration came from nothing but lies and what I thought was living. But God brought me to the police department to expose those things and now that I'm aware, I have accountability.

When conforming to this world, our mind tends to limit us as well make our ability to gain competency and achieve something only feel like a false bliss. I say that because I never saw anyone in my family in shape or working in a high professional job. Now when I talk about professionalism, I'm not talking about the way you act at a job, but how you take care of yourself.

I don't mean to put anyone down, but my bar came from seeing the men in the family with not very high standards. That's why I never reached for more or tried to better myself. I became so fearful of change and bettering myself that I started to become frustrated when I really wanted something .

My whole life I was looking to the world to validate myself, and I was failing with an empty feeling inside. Now I understand why God doesn't give us things when we are fearful, because it's the lack of faith in Him. God will not give you anything when you're fearful, because it won't work with you having a negative mindset.

Joining the police department, I had a terrible mindset at the beginning. My mindset had me defeated before any fitness test could do it. I admit I never thought I could get into shape; moreover, I was struggling with who I was as a person. My image of myself was so poor that what people thought of me was nowhere near what I thought of myself. It gets real in your head.

We bury our feelings with a victim mindset, looking for people to pat us on the back to get some kind of pleasure. What I mean by "pat on the back" is wanting someone to feel sorry for you. Our mind is easily persuaded due to how people are able to tap into our emotions. We often limit ourselves because we feel we're equal to the people were around, which in reality we're not. We are here not to please people, but God. Romans 12:2 talks about it. We lose because the world doesn't give us what we need, it only gives us what we want. But God gives you what you need and only for you to benefit from.

Before entering the Academy, we had orientation. Jesus! I forgot to pick up a field officer notebook. I was too scared to ask for a book because I didn't want to seem like a screw-up. Hell, I was the biggest guy "fat wise" in the class, and I knew people would look at me and start a conversation amongst themselves. During orientation, we received our benefits and our schedule of what we would be covering while in the Academy. Also, we had to purchase our gear: smirf uniforms and PT gear, along with other necessities.

Wrapping up the day, I picked up my paper work and gear to take home and prepare for my long week to get myself together. As I walked out the door, a officer pulled me over to the side and told me to finish. But with the doubt in my heart, I knew it would be a struggle because my conditioning wasn't up to par, and also my mental state wasn't good going into law enforcement. Mentally defeated – yeah, not a good start.

My first day at the Academy was a nightmare. June 08, 2020, at 6 a.m., the belt came on my ass and I was in for a rude awakening. The Drill Sergeant was all in my face, and they would discipline the whole class with push-ups and jumping jacks. Oh yeah, planks as well. I was exhausted and my thinking was all over the place.

Not once had I ever experienced a structure like that before. I mean, I played football, but it wasn't that intense. The hood mentality was far from what I was experiencing. Coaches at my high school did the bare minimum to keep us focused. In the hood where I'm from, sports was just a tool to keep us busy and out of trouble. Our coaches were great, but they weren't big on discipline, and a lot of our players weren't respectful. I can only imagine if some them were to talk to anybody in the LAPD like that, they would get a big surprise.

The Drill Sergeant's uniform was freshly pressed with the shiniest boots. I was amazed, but I had a face like humpty dumpty. What an embarrassment I displayed for myself and the Black race. Already I became a target not because of my skin, but because my actions.

I remembered that I had a bachelor's degree, but that didn't mean anything to them. I guess common sense ain't so common – I guess not for me. I couldn't even put my own paperwork in order. Before the end of my first day, one of the sergeants gave me a rude awakening.

My DI asked me a question and I didn't respond, not on purpose, but from being exhausted and got chewed out so much that my mind was in space. One of the sergeants got in my face and started yelling asking me to go home, but I didn't come to the Academy to go home. "This was my first day of greatness"

On my second day, we were preparing for our physical fitness test that required us to score an average of 50 percent or more to pass to continue on in the Academy. I went out there and landed a huge dump; my score was 17 percent, after which I felt terrible about myself. I wasn't the only one who failed, but damn, I didn't even come close to passing.

Honestly, 50 percent was the bare minimum, but at my age I should have been in the high 80's breezing through it. I know it wasn't fair to come out of shape, and when I failed I remembered all the times I shitted through life not taking anything seriously. It had all finally caught up to me. I could sense that I would be the talk around the Academy class, and I wasn't ready to hear the truth that I wasn't in shape.

At one time, I thought my size was okay – delusional, right, but that was the belief I brought with me going into the Academy. After I failed, I was asked to go see a nutritionist, and for first time I learned about what to eat.

Leading into the Academy, I struggled with writing. I would always get in trouble, so I would have to write 15:7 which was reports on what I did wrong. Honestly, my writing was so terrible that one of the DI's said I had the worst 15:7 she ever saw. I couldn't get mad, I could only agree silently. The truth hurt, and I could not blame anybody but myself. That was for all the time I barely got by in school. Never thought it would come back around and bite me in the ass. I thought being average would be okay, but you only get what you put in. That's why God takes things away from you, but if it's meant for you, He will give it back if you do the right thing.

God was able to get my attention from fitness to writing a simple sentence. Oh, yeah, my grammar and spelling were terrible. Those are areas that I have been struggling with my whole life. But, since getting closer to God, he was able to put people in my life to fix them.

I always had health insurance and every time I would see my doctor, he would strongly encourage me to go to the free nutrition class that Kaiser offered, but I never went because my mom would say you can be big and healthy. Yeah, parents, don't do that. If you have the opportunity to learn about good eating habits, I advise you to go. Many children are overweight here in America due to not knowing how to eat properly.

Going into my second week, we were introduced to our fire arms and tactics instructors at the Davis facility. There, we learned how to de-escalate situations before resorting to deadly force, and also what to do in dangerous situations. I admit during my firearms training, I struggled with remembering tactics; practicing firearms manipulation was hard because in my head I felt I didn't belong since I wasn't physically fit, so everything just felt like a waste of time.

During our time on the range, we would repeatedly go over how to properly draw our firearms. Sometimes I would point my firearm at a classmate intentionally. I knew the firearm instructor was questioning how the hell I got there, but I did, thanks.

This continued on until my final day of being in the Academy; however, during my last week we finally got a chance to shoot our guns. I started out doing bad, then toward the end I got a few shots on the target.

Before my last day, I meet with DI along with my Sergeant. They went over some bad peer evaluations from classmates. What was written about me – I didn't know many felt that way about me. I mean, some said things that I would have never said.

You'd think being in law enforcement, people would have some kind of positive thing to say, but I received a big pile of bad evaluations. Honestly, I knew it was going to happen. However, the truth is not meant to make you feel good, but to help you improve.

The class was only reacting to what they saw. I mean, if I had been in shape and confident, nobody would've said a damn thing. That was my wake-up call and God sending people to help me.

Going into my final week in the Academy, I was very nervous and was already defeated from jump. I just knew my conditioning wasn't up to par, but I was willing to go until the end. I would go to morning workouts and then do PT, but it didn't matter. I didn't have what it took. It was a hot Thursday morning at 3 a.m. I woke up to prepare for my final day with my 6-20 classmate. There was a lot of doubt in my mind and I didn't know how to motivate myself, so I thought about my family and my uncle that was killed, and how people saw me as hope.

Going into my final shot at passing the PFQ, I started crying because I didn't have what it took, but I took the test. After I finished the test, I waited for my DI to come back with the results and I learned I missed the PFQ by one point. I heard the news from my DI and it seemed like my hearing went bad. I was frozen and lost because I had to go home and face the music that I failed out of the Academy. I'd have to look at people that thought I would do well and explain to them that I failed.

Thank you, God, for sending me to the police department;. I know my experience wasn't so great, but I learned so much about myself in the process. I can never repay you guys for what you did for me. Before going through the process, I was a lost and overweight boy coming from a low-income single-parent home. Now, I appreciate where I'm from, but I have departure from you guys' train. I will never forget all the nice police officers that helped me along the way – too many to name, so I just want to thank everyone, regardless of whether our encounters were good or bad.

Joining was the beginning of a turnaround for me. Not just a career, but a way I could use my gifts to deal with people. I never got caught up in the money aspect, because when you have God, you'll never go broke. However, God placed me with LAPD to bring out the best in me. At home I wasn't my best and my health and diet were poor; my life was going bad. I couldn't stand to look at myself in the mirror at times. My sense of belonging was gone. I had trouble dealing with people. I was going through psychological warfare. Anyway, here's my journey to the man, Brent Palmer.

God saw me struggling and I realize that I had to make decision to do the right thing.

I thought I would never get back into the academy because the entry level examination was about to expire and they just changed the entry level test to multiple choice English. When I was calculating that up, I knew I was done. I never did well on any English exam.

Once I failed, I started clearing out my locker with the possession that I purchased. I then went to the DI office to return my san brown belt and gun. Returning the gun was the most hurtful part. I had to sign a lot of paperwork for my departure.

I talked to the sergeant and DI, and they encouraged me to get in shape and come back. But at the time I didn't want to hear that. I was hurt with a victim mentality. I let people overrule what I was supposed to be, which Is me. I came into the Academy with hopes that the LAPD would be my identity. I would get a chance to say I worked for the world famous Los Angeles Police Department.

I met with another sergeant that worked there, Sergeant C. I'm glad he stopped to talk to me. I was blessed, because two weeks later after I left, I was able to work out with him and he taught me how to eat and get my muscles stronger. I started losing a lot of weight and made tremendous progress toward my weight goal.

I changed the stores I shopped at. I started shopping at Trader Joes and Sprouts. I bought all organic fruits and vegetables. I lost 6 pounds within the first week. I thought I would end up looking like the "rock." Honestly, it was great feeling, I finally had someone to care and help me out. Being alone with no guidance is hard, I don't care what anyone says. Especially if you grow up in an environment that is consistently having the same negative results.

I started a "fit to hire" program; the class was designed to get future candidates ready for all the physical training. I did well, but not as well as I wanted. It was sad, because I would see my old classmates and I would get teary-eyed. I was embarrassed and felt the disconnection from never feeling a part of journey that was meant to achieve one goal, becoming a respectful police officer.

The fit to hire Classes were two days out of the week, Tuesday and Thursday, but due to my high demand job I had the opportunity to go one day out of the week. The class lasted for about a month until COVID stopped the classes.

One evening I went to the barbershop and I talked to my barber about what happen and he immediatley told me that he knew a retire cop. So, he gave me his number. I eventually called him and told him what happen, he asked me "how many miles were you running" I said 1. He replied, "Bruh, you need to be running five miles a day". Now remind you I never ran 1 straight mile. He eventually gave another candidates number Brother JJ that was in the process. I called him and we started workingout together. We would run three days out of the week, averaging 5 to 7 miles each time. He really pushed me like no other. He accepted me and took me in with open arms. He taught me how to run and also showed me what kind of shoes to buy. Before entering the Academy, I wore some Nike shoes like I was going to a pick-up basketball game. Ha! What a big mess I was.

I believe God brought us together to help each other out. He was also a product of single parenting; he shared the same struggle as me. It made sense, why we connected and stayed together. We also had mutual friends, so that was great. His family was good. We even went to San Diego together to try out for their police department, but I failed getting over the wall; he passed with flying colors.

I was happy for him – at least one of us made it. Months later, I retook the test and finally passed the second time, but was later turned down. I moved on and continued my process with the police department.

I was most fearful of the multiple choice test. I took the test once and didn't pass, and the victim mindset set came back. I wanted to blame people in the class and some of the DI that were in the Academy. I was looking for something to make me feel better about my bitch-ass mentality. I thought about quitting, but no one would give a damn.

No one knew my background, so the only thing that people picked on was me being quiet and not being assertive. Not passing the academy not only saved me from hurting myself, but for potentially hurting my partners. I wasn't ready. I would've hurt myself and my partner because of not being physically and mentally ready.

I went to Barnes & Noble and bought a dictionary and thesaurus. For a month straight, while at work I would look over at least 10 words and recite them and remember what they mean. Also, I would go on YouTube to look up how to properly use commas, semicolons, and colons; then I would practice writing sentences in my notebook so that I would remember better.

That was first time I took English seriously. It felt like I was studying for the SAT. All that work paid off; I took the test and finally passed, with a sigh of relief. I started seeing the change at work. I was actually putting in the work. I felt so great that I got a tattoo.

I learned when you ask God to give you the power, He will give it to you…you just have to put in the work. No one is going to give you anything; however, no racism, person, or family member can keep you from what God has for you. Remember and trust that.

Many people like to brag about their power, but don't talk about what is really going on with them. You ever notice someone who always needs to show off what they have instead of wanting to show who they really are? It's because they are really have nothing outside of what they have. I used to put people before God when I got hurt, but not anymore. I can have what I want, and I mean *whatever I want,* without the approval of people. Just have to put the work in and be sincere and not half ass doing the job.

I don't blame unfairness or people's judgement about me; I took responsibility and I fixed everything that was wrong with me. I also notice how I cared about others opinion of me and not God's opinion of me; that was me conforming to the world, not appreciating the beautiful man that I was. You have to understand that the world will take advantage of you, not just physically but mentally.

Being in the Academy, I learned no matter your rank or title that makes you feel higher than the next person, it can never equal the character that you possess as an individual. Character is what keeps genuine love around you, not the money that attracts people for all the wrong reasons. Because when you leave the world; the people you encountered will always remember how you made them feel emotionally.

No amount of material possessions can ever leave an imprint on anyone's mind like the love you give to them. No valuables like clothes, cars, and jewelry can ever replace character, because all those man-made things get old and eventually end up in the dumpster or with someone else, because the value has run out. But the things we leave in a person's heart will forever be the foundation of genuine love.

The man has finally come out of the shell. I'm no longer afraid to be comfortable in my own skin as an individual. Why have something when you're not ready or too afraid to have it? I feel good knowing that everything that has happened to me has been of great benefit to me. As an African American male here in America, I share with you this: Nobody can keep you down but yourself. I no longer listen to the world that wants you to feel like them. I'm my own man, and I will be the best person I can be. Being Black is not hard; it's a beautiful experience that I learned to embrace with pride. I used to think it's too damn hard to be Black, but today I no longer think that. The world has no power over you, but if you fall victim to it, it will! I'am beyond proud of the Brent Palmer, and nobody on this earth can make me feel anything less. Now, "Can you dig that sucka?" - Booker T.

On July 6th 2022 at 0600 hours, I, recruit officer Palmer made my return to the Los Angeles police department. What a moment it was seeing everybody again, not knowing what to expect. My first day was considered hell day, but by the looks of things everybody was chill.

My third day, we had a PFA test that did not determine whether your job would be on the line or not. I killed it. When we did group runs, I was able to keep up and strive. All thanks to God and people that he put in my life to help me transform.

Academically, I was passing my exams and doing fair with tactics and firearms. The only thing that I lacked was having a big voice. Not sure how people felt about me in the Academy, but I met a few people who became really cool friends: Officers Lopez and both Stephanie Martinez, three people I will never forget. The bond we shared was almost like God put us together for a reason.

Arcon sessions were great. I was able to display my techniques as well show people that I would put my hands on someone. HA! "Insider". Moving along, I went through the Academy with flying colors without being on academic probation, proving that I could pass any test thrown at me.

First round in the Academy. I remember leaving and telling God to take control of my life, and He did. I witnessed hardwork, working 12 hour shifts lifting heavy boxes six days a week. I learned what sacrifice was. Not only that, but the small price that I had to pay in order to be great, and when I talk about great, I don't mean beating my chest, but great in being a good human being - healthy, taking care of my temple. That was the greatest gift I can ever receive.

God showed me who we are as people. Unfortunately we have fallen; however, once we accept God, He brings us back to glory. Glory not in wanting to control over others, but in being a family and having respect for one another again. I went through a lot, and I overcame doubting myself and not liking myself.

I sacrificed so that my family members can live. First I was living for myself, life is not about us no matter how badly we want to live a lavish life. It's amazing how one year can change your whole life, including your family's life. I can see the change in my family. I have family members working full-time jobs and also becoming healthier.

On December 17, 2021 at approximately 0800 hour, I Brent Palmer earn my right to be called a Police Officer. All the hardwork paid off and I was able to redefine my life by doing what was right and changing within.

I would like to thank my brother lopez and both Steph, you guys are the G.O.A.T! also I would like to thank the entire Police Academy staff, you guys are appreciated. To Officer G, I will get you some soul food.

FOOTBALL COACH

Tookie Williams

As I watched your movie, "Redemption," I couldn't help but notice the hurt in your eyes when you were being interviewed about your father; how things would've been different had you had that role model in your life. What would you have been? Who knows? You turned your pain into smoke, your anger into fists, and that led to you crashing down on people that look like you. Imagine if you had that father cheering you on, leading you into light? Instead, you walked into a place with nothing good to reference from.

The world took advantage of you and called you a monster. Unfortunately your life ended before you had the chance to live right on the free side. Your life was robbed by the lack of knowledge from your father. You were not a murderer, drug user, or a pimp – you're a human being. It suck the world used you. Who you were in your dark days is no longer valid; what's most important is the hurt that led you down that road. Rest well.

Brent Palmer

In 2014, I wrapped up my football career at my junior College with hopes of playing at the collegiate level, but later came to the realization that it would not happen due to me being too short and extremely big. I couldn't change position unless I lost weight, but that wasn't going to happen because I was too lazy to lose the weight. The victim mindset took over so much that I didn't have hope.

I would always reference hard work, but didn't do it. I just wanted to show social media that I was doing something. I was afraid to hurt, because I didn't like the feeling of hurting. Being comfortable and content was where I wanted to be, because I didn't have anything to work hard for. I thought about my myself and no one else, so quitting and giving half effort was fine with me.

One day I decided to go back to my old high school to visit my old coach. At first, I volunteered my time and then was asked if I wanted to help out. At first I was hesitant, but later broke down and agreed to coach. I remember being slightly excited, because I would be helping kids and I wanted to teach them like my senior year high school coach taught me.

First day stepping out in the field, I saw myself again, but this time through the kids I was about to coach. Some were out of shape, some had questions on their faces about how practice would be going. A child displaying outrageous behavior could be so powerful but yet misunderstood by many. For example, at practice when a kid would talk to me in a disrespectful manner, I would see their interaction with their mothers and I'd see why they carried themselves like that.

Now I realize why kids act out – because they are crying out for help and they're looking for direction from anywhere when they are lost in this big world full temptations and uncertainty. I realize the power of genuine love and how it grows a flower even when it's in 100 degree's heat. Being a coach, I was able to see the problems that go on with kids acting tough only because they don't know anything else but to act like that. Yes, kids are aware of their actions; however, we must look at a teaching point. If all you know is chaos, then that's all you know. You can't beat a kid, but you can hold them accountable after you teach them the right way.

I cry every year because of the impact that I made on the kids year in and year out. I feel good knowing that I was more than a coach, but a person who showed them that there is a better way than your block and being an average student. Take me for example. I was a complete dumbass and was alway looking to play the victim, so it was easy for me to feel sorry for myself and act out when I knew damn well I shouldn't be acting like that. It was my only way of having some kind of visibility in the world and to my peers. I don't wish to pass that legacy on to my kids. Moving along…

When you see a kid – his character, diet, and demeanor – you see his home "parenting." We often judge children based on their behavior. However, there is a pattern and teaching that the kid has learned and picked up on. We see how parents can either damage or evaluate their children. For example, my mom always talked about how hard it is out here, and I wouldn't see her want more. Also, our diet was poor. We were basically eating to survive instead of eating to live.

What I learned as an adult is if you don't put in the work, you will not move. No matter how much you pray, you will still be in the same place. Many kids fall for "the world is hard" slogan because their parents choose not to change their lives, not because they don't want to, but they simply don't want to make the effort to change.

As explained in my first chapter, when children don't have the proper guidance, they tend to act out in a subconscious manner. Teaching and coaching, I was able to detect behaviors based on observation. Do we blame the kids who is learning his way around the world by his environment outside of home, or do we look to the parents and put the responsibility on them?

Many parents suffer in silence, which is why they act out in an unpleasant way at home toward their children. For example, growing up I saw my mom being angry at dad and for some reasons I didn't understand at the time, and I saw us having terrible eating habits because we were eating to survive, not to live. These were the things that had me following in the same footsteps, which later developed a man with poor moral values and understanding of how to properly function as a man in the world.

That, I believe, is why children like rappers and jewelry – because it hides who they really are. It makes them look successful, but inside that little boy is crying and seeking help, but doesn't know where to go.

Lastly, our parents can limit us in a way that society can ever do. Growing up, I saw my mom living a mediocre life: Social Security check, odd jobs, and government assistance. I once thought that was the only thing I could do as far as making a living and being able to provide for a family. Boy was I wrong. That mindset kept me from thinking more of myself, which led to me eating and wanting to do nothing with myself.

There was a time I told myself I couldn't wait to graduate high school so that I could get a Social Security check and not have to punch the clock. What a toxic and un-manly way of thinking that was; no good woman will ever put up with that.

Now I see people are comfortable around certain people because they're thinking the same way. Children tend to mimic what their parents do, and when you see a child's behavior and get to know their parents, you see why the cycle continues and it doesn't get better.

Not having a positive relationship or image of a family at home, children tend to lean toward what they see outside of home. And when dealing with the world, many conform to the world and lose themselves in the process. For example, in high school I acted like I was someone else. I thought that by acting that way people would genuinely like me, but once I got older, I realized that I was living for the world and not my true character. As you can see, life catches up to you and when you're not who you say you are, eventually you'll break down to who you really are.

What I learned from coaching football was how important having a father figure in your life is, and how a kid's mind Is constantly seeking answers. With that being said, I would like to take the time out to talk about that many things that were revealed to me while coaching.

I'll start with the lack of a father in the kid's life. Some kids were rebellious and had a hard time paying attention to me. I learned that the only authority figure that ever talked to them like that was their mother. My respect goes out to the mothers that are raising a man on their own. I know it's not easy and to my Queens, you're appreciated.

Even though I was only 20 years old when I started coaching, I had a huge effect on kids, as If I was a father. Remember, I was raised in a single-parent home and I understand the struggle of finding your way in a world that has little patience for kids and their problems.

School just assumes that the kids have a terrible upbringing at home, but they fail to realize that the kids' self-esteem and confidence are shattered because they have no one to look up to. However, I discovered that with love and genuine attention, kids will listen and learn. I don't mean learning football plays, but developing character that they never knew was there.

As kids, we think character is fucking a hundred girls at school or at home while our parents are gone. But true character is being yourself in spite of what the world tells you to become. That's why you see so many kids leaning toward what everybody else does, such as drugs, scaming, and failing out of school. These behaviors lead to prison – not only physical prison, but mental prison as well.

I believe mental prison is worse than physical prison, because if you don't have your own my mind then someone else does. The world is full of temptations, which can lead down roads that can be dark and not for us.

Kids are rebellious toward adults because of the lack of respect they have for them. Kids know when you mean them well, and they know when you're full of shit. Back to character, character is everything, because without it, you will be living a lie.

I often see parents talk about why their kid is so out of control, then you look at their life at home. You see the mother dating guys who doesn't work and disrespect them, so the kid ends up becoming rebellious toward the mom because she don't have respect for herself.

Here are examples that I experienced within my family: Women sleeping around with men and not married; the women having men use them and disrespect them. I would like to point out "you are what you attract." I said that to say you can't want respect from a child if you don't have respect for yourself. That's why kids become angry toward their parents.

Well, that's what I came up with. Being a coach, I was able to show genuine care and I led by example. I worked while going to school full time, as well caring for them. That's why I was able to connect and penetrate kids' minds.

Through coaching, you see the lack of respect kids have for parents, and meeting some I see why. When you don't respect yourself, how can a kid respect you? For example, I saw my uncle raise his kids and when he would try to discipline them, they would be rebellious. Now at that time, I thought they were being disrespectful because my mom would say these kids nowadays are disrespectful. I realized kids know when they are in a fucked up environment and it shows in their behavior.

When kids have support and a healthy environment, they excel and do really well. When I was in the Police Academy, I didn't have the greatest support at home. I don't mean money, but the energy and people having the same mindset of wanting you to excel at your goal. Family cycles tend to linger around when kids constantly pick on the same bullshit such as low grades, poor health, and negative character. These are the things that cause the downfall of children.

Another thing I've noticed is that children are scared to talk about their emotions, which is why later on they disconnect from people like their family and friends. I had the same problem growing up, because I felt like I didn't have anybody to talk to. However, I used to write down things that were going on in my head to kind of empty out my loneliness. I never had a dad to talk with about personal stuff, and I didn't feel comfortable talking about it with my mom. So, when I hurt I would display it through being silent or distant from people. I created that behavior based on not being able to talk about it at home, so being shy was my personality. It was like I didn't know how to function in the world.

Most men won't admit their shortcomings or their embarrassing moments in life, due to the fact that the world will label them as soft or not manly. These are the things men go through, which later lead to them not solving their problems and eventually going through life not living for themselves. What I mean by that is, men tend to put on an act in order to fit in. That's why you see so many people trying to act the same instead of being themselves.

The world has a big influence on our daily lives; if it didn't, we wouldn't be in so much competition. Why is it when we walk out the door, we measure ourselves by what we have or drive? Why can't it be a simple "Hey, how are you doing?" without having to feel like we have something to prove?

Kids fight over Jordans to impress friends who could care less about them. Those Jordans will not build your character. When those things are gone, can you still be happy and treat people with respect, or will you still smile to others? I mean, these are the things that we don't think of when we have things covering up our character. What happens to genuine friendship?

The world has covered our feelings with material things that we become blind to in our own lives. I remember my mom would buy me shoes and I couldn't wait to stunt on friends at school, but little did they know I was hurting and looking for validation to pump myself up. I became so blind to wanting recognition that my health was failing and my character was being tarnished by my own foolishness.

When a kid feels loved and has the proper care, he will prosper in a way that no one will imagine. When children are behaving badly toward you, it's because deep down he wants parents to talk to him and guide him through life.

Positive self-image comes from your parents, and those who don't have that image at home tend to lean toward the world for their image; however, that is not what God made us to do. God made everyone for their own purpose of life. I believe many children struggle with their image growing up due to lack of parenting at home.

Some children have better relationships with their friends than their own parents. For example, when I would go to school, I would try to be like others and not myself, mainly because I wasn't learning how to be a man at home. Consciously I knew when I was making the wrong decision, because it would always begin to bother my conscience, but this behavior would condition your mind to think that this is the proper way of thinking.

I would like to point out how important having a father figure in a male's life. It lays the foundation for a child's image. Without that, kids tend to gain their self-worth through the approval of the world. Not once did I think to ask my mom why my dad was never there.

A lot of single women are raising kids. That was what I saw in my family so it just felt normal, until I'd see some kids at school with their mom *and* dad. It felt weird in a way, because I wanted to know what it was like to have your father supporting you and teaching you how to treat a woman.

There were many questions I had that I was too afraid to ask my mom; I thought they were too personal or soft. For example, having a male erection – I used to think my penis was going through something, but it was an experience that every male experiences. These are small things that turn out to be big things later on. Oftentimes, kids become distant from parenting because they never had anyone to talk to.

Single moms, stay encouraged. Learn to uplift yourself as a woman and learn not to become bitter. Don't start feeling like you're not worthy of love; continue to get better and you will attract better.

Too many times I see a mom raising three kids and taking it out on the children subconsciously. I say that because I experienced how my mom would get mad at me and compare my behavior to my dad. So Queens, elevate and become the woman for your King, and keep God first. I thought I could live my life my way, until God started whooping my ass and I felt miserable about everything I did. Once I let Him lead, my life I started to prosper. Think big and never doubt your ability to overcome any circumstance.

When is it okay for men to express themselves comfortably without feeling less than a man? I struggled with this question while I was growing up. I thought acting macho was the way to go, but all it created was a soft man outside that pretended to be hard. For instance, I walked around with my chest out like I'm the guy to be, the way I talked and dressed.

I would act out in class because I was a true dumbass. That was my way of getting people to see me as somebody. In first grade, I remember my teacher would have us read aloud and I knew I wasn't that good, so as soon as my turn would come around, I would start acting like an ass. This made my teacher think I had ADHD. My mother had a meeting with her to discuss some of the issues I was having, but no matter what they were talking about, I knew what my problem was and I was too afraid to ask for help. How would I feel asking for help, "I'm a man" in my head. I used acting out to cover my lack of ability to be competent.

I'm here to tell you that it is okay to express yourself freely on how you feel. There is no right or wrong way to express yourself. If I had a chance to do it all over again, I would've been more open to talking about my days and feelings with people, but society dictated my thoughts on how I was supposed to act. Here is my wonderful journey through being a boy fighting to become a man through multiple struggles.

Thank God for COVID saving my life. 2019 was the beginning of something great for me, saving the lost boy. The LAPD saved me from obesity and exposed me. It was lonely getting my shit together, but I got through and I will forever be grateful.

As I looked around and saw how many use the system as way to stay at home, I was grinding and working on myself. If I hadn't joined, I woud have been like the majority of my peers, lazy and thinking of the next scam to get by. When I mean scam I don't mean the internet, but next victim mind episode.

I still remember when my mother made me get on "General Relief", the feeling of being comfortable not having to work. I remember walking into the building with people who looked homeless and people who were young and healthy. I knew they could work; I had no clue what was going on, I just knew I was about get free money and not have to work for It.

I will like to take the time out to thank everyone who helped me in my time of need. Starting with my entire family, I wrote this because the struggle ended with me and I must admit I took the punishment so that the future kids could be free.

Secondly I would like to thank my friends Wil, Marquise, Eduardo, Dabai, Mr. Poole, Cortez, Destiney, Ree, Tatierria, thank you guys for all the support and love.

Thirdly I would like to thank LAPD for accepting me and helping along the way. I just had to come back and let God show out one time. There are to many to name, but those who know me know that you're loved.

To my barber Zo thanks for having a listen ear.

Anyways stay up little solider their will be better days. The key to success is treating your bad days and good days the same. From Compton with love

Printed in the United States
by Baker & Taylor Publisher Services